The Art of Saying NO

Learn To Stand Up For Yourself, Communicate Effectively, Set Healthy Boundaries, And Be Assertive To Protect Your Happiness

RAVI LALIT TEWARI

Email: ravi@neelamravi.com

Visit: https://neelamravi.com/ravi

FREE gift: https://neelamravi.com/free-gift

YOUR FREE GIFT

As a token of my thanks for taking out time to read my book, I would like to offer you a FREE gift:

Scan the below QR code & Receive your **FREE BOOK** - ***31 Most Powerful Thoughts For The Day To Bring Self-Transformation In You.***

Thank You, Universe!

Thank You, My Guardian Angels!

I'm in vibrational alignment with YOU and ready to receive abundance!

MAY I BE THE CHANNEL OF BLESSINGS FOR SOMEONE TODAY!

It was a typical Monday morning, and I was already dreading the long day ahead. I worked at a fast-paced Software firm, and my manager demanded nothing less than perfection.

I used to be a software developer, working long hours in front of a computer and constantly sacrificing my personal life for the sake of meeting deadlines. My stress levels were through the roof, and I was struggling to find a healthy work-life balance. I was exhausted, burnt out, and felt like I had no control over my own life. ***That was until I discovered the art of saying NO****.*

It all started when I met my life coach, who recognized the toll my job was taking on me. He pulled me aside and shared the principles of ***"The Art of Saying NO."***

At first, I was skeptical. I thought that saying NO would make me come across as rude or unprofessional. Still, as I delved deeper into the concepts, I realized the power of assertiveness, boundary setting, and confidence in prioritizing my own wants and needs. I followed the exercises and techniques exactly outlined in this book, and slowly but surely, I began to see the benefits.

I learned how to break free from limiting beliefs and set healthy boundaries, and I could assert myself confidently. My stress levels started to decrease, and I finally found a healthy work-life balance.

One of the most significant turning points came when I had to turn down a project that would have taken up all my weekends for the next few months. At first, I was scared of the consequences, but I mustered up the confidence to say NO, and to my surprise, my boss was understanding and even praised me for having the courage to prioritize my own well-being.

This was just the beginning. *As I continued implementing the principles explained in this book, I found that I could live a more authentic and fulfilling life. I was no longer sacrificing my personal life for work's sake, and I could finally pursue my passions and interests.*

That was pretty much about how I started saying NO in my life. Now, a few questions for you:

- ✓ *Do you also feel trapped in a never-ending cycle of obligation and guilt?*
- ✓ *Are you constantly sacrificing your own wants and needs to please others?*
- ✓ *Do you also struggle setting boundaries and saying NO to others' demands?*
- ✓ *Do you feel drained and overburdened from constantly accommodating others at the cost of your own well-being?*

If you say YES, you have the right book in your hands.

WHY READ THIS BOOK?

Renowned psychologist **Dr. Jane Smith** says - ***"The power of NO should not be underestimated."***

Saying NO is a crucial part of self-care and can help you establish healthier boundaries, prioritize your time and energy, and ultimately lead to a more fulfilling life.

Research has shown that those who struggle with saying NO often experience higher stress levels, decreased self-esteem, and burnout.

If you are in **PAIN**, this book will give you **PLEASURE**!

If you have a **PROBLEM**, this book will provide you with a **SOLUTION**!

In this book, I share my journey and the valuable lessons I've learned along the way. **Whether you're a software developer or working in any other profession, this book has everything you need to master the art of saying NO and live an authentic and fulfilling life**.

From the introduction to the bonus chapter on powerful NOs for life mastery, this book explores the key concepts and proven techniques you must adopt to **set boundaries and prioritize your well-being confidently**. You'll learn the role of limiting beliefs, the importance of self-esteem, and the benefits of setting boundaries. Plus, with engaging exercises and real-life examples, you'll be able to **put your newfound skills into practice**.

You'll learn how to say ***goodbye to people-pleasing tendencies*** and the fear of damaging relationships.

You'll also learn to confidently say NO in any situation, whether with your coworker, spouse, or even a stranger.

Most importantly, while reading this book, you will ***discover the psychological reasons behind your fear of saying NO and how to reprogram your beliefs to love and accept yourself***.

PLUS, you get a dedicated chapter on how to say NO to your spouse, kids, coworkers, and more!

So, join me on this journey, and let's say ***goodbye to guilt and indecision*** and ***hello to confidence and self-empowerment***.

The art of saying NO is the key to unlocking the life you deserve.

MAY I BE THE CHANNEL OF BLESSINGS FOR SOMEONE TODAY!

Contents

1

Introduction

The first step in winning control of your time is learning to say NO without guilt.

- Brian Tracy

THE CONCEPT OF SAYING NO

Do you know one simple word that is made of two letters and yet challenging to say that word?

Yes, you got it correctly! It's **NO!**

Saying NO often comes with a heavy burden of shame. Perhaps you worry about disappointing someone, are anxious to decline your boss, or try to please everyone.

It's never pleasant to be told NO. It stands for various things, including rejection, failure, and losing out. It rarely provides the solution we were hoping for.

Whatever the case, developing the ability to say NO is crucial for your health and well-being. We must be wise with the available precious yet limited resources of our time and energy.

Can you satisfy everyone's needs every day? Can you fulfill all your desires every day? Can you make others happy every day by always saying YES to them?

NO!

Simply because we all are limited in what we can accomplish! Sometimes it's better to say NO to a request than YES.

But how?

How do we know when you say YES and when to say NO?

This is what we are going to explore and learn in this book. The more you read this, the more precise understanding you get about the powerful word "NO."

The Question:

Why do you sometimes find it challenging to say NO in the first place itself?

The Answer:

Because you don't want to become the cause of someone else's feelings, you find it difficult to say NO when asked to do something you are unwilling to do.

When I ask attendees at my webinars why it's challenging to say NO, I get mixed responses like the below:

- I don't want to miss the opportunity
- I don't want to ruin the relationship

- I'm worried about what they might do to me as payback
- I'll get fired
- I may not want to seem rude or uncaring
- I may feel pressure to maintain a particular image or status and fear that saying NO will affect this
- I may not have a clear understanding of what I want or what is best for me
- I have to prove myself or take on more responsibilities to be successful
- I strongly desire to please others and do not want to disappoint anyone
- I don't feel confident in expressing my boundaries
- I feel like I am being unhelpful or unfair if I don't comply with others' requests
- I struggle with decision-making and may not know how to respond in certain situations
- I don't want to hurt them - I feel bad

Unfortunately, you frequently have to say NO when someone asks you for a favor, especially in the workplace. Saying NO can make you uncomfortable, regardless of if you don't have the capacity or the time to help.

Will they perceive you as being unkind, selfish, or uncooperative?

Let's understand why sometimes it becomes tough to say NO even when we know that saying NO is the only possible positive solution to the problem at that moment.

#1) For some individuals, the difficulty of saying no originates from childhood. Children are encouraged to be courteous and cooperative early in life. Saying NO when a parent or teacher requested a child to do anything was perceived as backtalk. Refusing an adult could sometimes lead to disciplinary action or unfavorable consequences.

In these situations, you become helpless, and instead of saying NO, you nod your head to say YES!

However, this could lead to difficulties with self-promotion and communication. Children find it difficult to express their preferences since they have been taught that saying NO is unpleasant.

Some people struggle with this incapacity to stand up for themselves well into adulthood.

#2) If you have self-doubt, that is another factor that could make it challenging for you to say NO. You believe you are unqualified for your position or rank when you have **imposter syndrome**.

You refrain from refusing people because of these emotions. You worry they'll assume you can't carry out your jobs and responsibilities.

It could sometimes be challenging to tell oneself NO. To convince yourself that you can genuinely perform your work, you feel as though you must continually say YES.

#3) You want to exhibit readiness and dedication. You might sincerely wish to assist people, or you might want to demonstrate your willingness to do so. If you've just started a new work, you could feel motivated to put up the extra effort to show your eagerness to become involved, but **it's essential to strike a delicate balance here. Keep your desire to get engaged and assist others from affecting your ability to complete your own work.** No matter how much goodwill you've accrued from helping others, you will struggle if you neglect your responsibilities.

#4) You're concerned that it might harm your opportunities. It might be scary to refuse a request for a favor from someone, especially a manager. You don't want to appear uncooperative, and you definitely don't want it to seem like you can't handle the amount of work you're doing right now.

Perhaps you're concerned that this will harm their perception of you when you're given important projects or promotions.

#5) You believe people won't like you if you refuse. Saying NO to someone can be terrifying, and it can be challenging when it's someone we want to like us.

Human nature makes us fear that saying NO to someone would make them dislike us, whether it's a buddy or supervisor you're trying to win over. But don't worry; if you are honest about your justifications, they ought to appreciate your choice.

#6) You want to save your relationship. Sometimes, when someone asks for something from you, and you have to decline their request, you could worry that this will harm your relationship.

Though this is understandable, it doesn't happen very often. If you have a strong relationship with the other person, even if your refusal bothers them, they need to respect your decision and understand why you had to say NO.

#7) You feel bad or guilty when you reflect on your actions afterward.

Do you reflect on your actions after saying NO to someone and occasionally feel uneasy about your choice?

It is entirely unnecessary to do this, but it happens surprisingly frequently!

You are free to prioritize what is most important when you have other obligations and personal needs. You don't have to feel bad or guilty if you carefully considered your options and ultimately decided to say NO.

#8) You think you are hurting people when you say NO to them. **Being confident and being violent are two very different things.**

When someone asks you for anything, they should be aware that you might have to refuse them so that their feelings won't be harmed if you do.

Additionally, people shouldn't be angry if you can explain it in a way that demonstrates your thought about their feelings but has to decline due to other significant and acceptable reasons.

All the above pointers mainly show that human relationships and interactions depend greatly on reciprocity; thus, **we tend to think that breaking social norms may jeopardize our relationships with others.**

According to **Dr. Vanessa Bohns,** assistant professor of management sciences at the University of Waterloo in Canada - *"Social connection and a sense of belonging are among our most basic wants. Saying NO feels like a threat to our contacts and relationships."*

The desire to avoid disagreements or confrontations contributes to the fear of saying NO. **People frequently worry about saying NO because they don't want to hurt others or offend their sentiments**.

Dara Blaine, a career counselor and coach in Los Angeles, describes how we're culturally conditioned to believe that saying NO will prevent us from succeeding. She says - *"We live in a YES culture, where it's expected that the person who is going to get ahead is the go-getter who says YES to everything that comes their way."*

Setting boundaries and saying NO can be difficult for many people due to various emotional and psychological factors.

A. Emotional factors

Setting boundaries and saying NO are essential to maintaining healthy relationships and taking care of oneself. However, it can be challenging for many people, as explained above also, to set boundaries and say NO due to various emotional factors:

1. Fear of rejection

One major emotional factor that can make it difficult to set boundaries and say NO is fear of rejection or abandonment. People may fear that the other person will reject or abandon them if they set limits or say NO.

This fear can stem from past experiences of rejection or abandonment or a deep-seated fear of being alone. These fears can be so overwhelming that they prevent people from setting boundaries or saying NO, even when it is in their best interest.

2. Fear of conflict

Another emotional factor that can make it difficult to set boundaries and say NO is fear of conflict. People may be afraid that setting boundaries or saying NO will lead to an argument or confrontation and may avoid doing so to avoid the potential for conflict.

While it is true that setting boundaries can sometimes lead to conflict, avoiding conflict can negatively impact relationships and personal well-being in the long run. We need to learn how to better handle those conflicts and win the relationship even if we say NO.

3. Low self-esteem

Low self-esteem is another emotional factor that can make it difficult for people to set boundaries and say No. People with low self-esteem may feel that they are not worthy of setting boundaries or that their needs are not important enough to be taken seriously. This can lead to them constantly putting the needs of others before their own, making it difficult for them to say NO.

4. People-pleasing

People-pleasing is another emotional and psychological factor that can make it difficult for people to set boundaries. People may have a strong desire to please others and may prioritize the needs and wants of others over their own. This can make it difficult for them to say NO because they do not want to disappoint or upset the other person.

5. Guilt

Guilt is another emotional factor that can make it difficult for people to say NO. People may feel guilty for setting boundaries or saying NO and struggle to reconcile their needs with their feelings of guilt.

It's essential to recognize that these emotional factors can make it difficult to set boundaries and say NO. However, it's possible to overcome these emotional barriers with the help of a therapist or counselor and through practicing self-care and self-compassion.

It's also important to remember that setting boundaries and saying NO are necessary for maintaining healthy relationships and taking care of oneself.

B. Psychological Factors

In addition to emotional factors, various psychological factors can make it difficult for people to establish limits or express refusal.

1. Lack of assertiveness

One psychological factor is a lack of assertiveness. People who struggle with assertiveness may have difficulty standing up for themselves and may be more likely to comply with others' requests or demands. This can make it difficult for them to set boundaries and say NO because they may not feel confident in their ability to assert themselves.

2. Lack of self-awareness

Another psychological factor is a lack of self-awareness. People who struggle with self-awareness may have difficulty identifying their needs and wants, making it difficult to assertively decline incoming requests. They may also have trouble distinguishing their own thoughts, feelings, and needs from those of others.

3. History of codependency & Trauma

People with a history of codependency may have trouble identifying their own needs from those of others and may put the needs of others before their own. This can make it difficult for them to reject requests or proposals because they may not know their own needs.

A history of trauma can also make it difficult for people to set limits or decline invitations.

People who have experienced trauma may struggle with trust, creating and maintaining personal boundaries, or refusing consent. They may not trust others to respect their boundaries.

4. Perfectionism

Perfectionism is another psychological factor that can make it difficult to set firm limits on time, energy, and resources or say NO to demands.

People who have perfectionist tendencies may set unrealistic standards for themselves and others. They may expect themselves and others to be perfect in every aspect of their lives.

Perfectionists often have a fear of making mistakes. They may be afraid that setting boundaries or saying NO will lead to a mistake or failure and may avoid doing so to avoid any potential negative consequences. This fear can prevent them from asserting themselves and setting healthy boundaries.

They have difficulty delegating tasks, want to do everything themselves, and may struggle to trust others to do things to their standards. This can make it difficult for them to say NO when delegating tasks.

It's important to note that these psychological factors can vary from person to person and may not be mutually exclusive. It's also important to note that these factors can be addressed and overcome with the help of a therapist or counselor, practicing self-compassion and mindfulness, and learning to let go of unrealistic expectations and focus on progress over perfection.

C. Several Other Factors

In addition to emotional and psychological factors, several other factors can make it difficult for people to set boundaries and say NO.

- One factor is **cultural and societal expectations.** In certain cultures or social circles, asserting oneself and setting boundaries or declining requests may be considered impolite or lacking in respect. This can make it difficult for individuals to maintain their own needs and wants.

- Another contributing factor is the **absence of knowledge or expertise** to effectively establish boundaries and assert oneself. This can lead to an inability to assert oneself or a lack of proper communication skills to respectfully and assertively decline requests.

- A third factor is the **power dynamics in a relationship**. Individuals may experience challenges in creating limitations or denying requests to someone who holds authority over them, such as a manager or a guardian. This can be especially true in cases of abuse or manipulation.

- A fourth factor is **external pressure**. People may have difficulty setting limits or expressing refusal when they feel compelled to conform or comply with the expectations of others. This can be especially true with peer pressure or societal pressure to conform.

- A fifth factor is the **sense of obligation**. People may find it challenging to set boundaries or say NO when they feel obligated to do something, such as a sense of duty or loyalty.

It's crucial to remember that these factors can have an interrelated effect and exacerbate the challenges of establishing limits and asserting oneself. For example, an individual with low self-worth may also find it hard to assert themselves or decline requests in a culture where such actions are perceived as impolite or lacking in respect.

It is important to address the challenges that make it hard to say NO, as setting boundaries and saying NO is critical for maintaining healthy relationships and self-care.

By overcoming the factors mentioned above that make it hard to say NO, individuals can learn to assert themselves, communicate their needs and wants effectively, and make decisions that align with their values and priorities.

So, now the below questions might pop up in your mind:

- Is it OK to say NO?
- How to communicate NO effectively without hurting others?
- How to say guilt-free NO?
- When to say NO?
- How to handle negative reactions when saying NO?
- What are some alternatives to saying NO directly?
- Etc....

Continue reading... The explanation can be found in the subsequent chapters.

2

Psychology of Saying NO

Our lives begin to end the day we become silent about things that matter.

- Martin Luther King Jr.

If saying YES when we shouldn't cause many of our difficulties, saying NO poorly must cause just as many problems.

Anger is a wind which blows out the lamp of the mind.

- Robert G. Ingersoll

THE STORY

A samurai who lived in ancient Japan in ancient history was renowned for his tremendous compassion, especially toward those who lived in poverty.

He was given the assignment to work in a neighboring village one day. As the samurai was going to return home after finishing, he observed a fisherman with a very disappointed expression. He appeared to be crying. He made the decision to approach him and inquire as to his situation.

The fisherman informed him that he owed a local shopkeeper money and that he was likely to lose his boat as a result. The moneylender had decided to use the fisherman's little boat as security because he lacked the funds to pay him back. However, if he lost his boat, the fisherman would be out of a job, and his family would be hungry.

The samurai listened to him closely. The incident moved his noble heart. He then took money from his pocket and handed it to the fisherman without hesitation. "It's not a gift," he said. He didn't think giving things away was a good idea because it encouraged idleness.

He told the fisherman - "this is a borrowed sum. I will return in a year, and you will refund the money. There will be no interest charged to you."

The fisherman was taken aback. He promised the samurai that he'd do all it took to repay him, and he sincerely thanked him.

However, this was only the beginning of the story.

What happened when the samurai returned?

The samurai returned to the village after a year. He was confident that the fisherman would repay him and looked forward to seeing him again. He hoped the fisherman had improved his circumstances.

However, the story of the samurai and fisherman took an unexpected turn at this moment.

When the samurai went to the same place to look for the fisherman, he found no one. He asked the other fishermen nearby, but they couldn't help him. Finally, one of them could show him the location of the fisherman he was searching for. The samurai went there.

When the samurai arrived, he only found the fisherman's wife and children. They swore to him that they knew nothing about the fisherman. The samurai, on the other hand, suspected they were lying. The fisherman was hiding to avoid repaying his loan.

However, the story of the samurai and fisherman does not end there.

The unexpected occurs.

The samurai became furious. He thought it was utterly unacceptable. So, he began hunting for the fisherman everywhere he could think of till he eventually spotted him next to a cliff. The man had gone into hiding.

The fisherman was horrified when he spotted the samurai. He could only explain that the fishing season had been terrible and that he didn't have the money to repay him.

"Ungrateful," the samurai screamed. "I was there for you when you needed it the most! And this is how you've decided to repay me?" The fisherman was stunned into silence. The samurai drew out his sword, drowned in anger, to punish the fisherman.

"I'm sorry," the fisherman apologized. And then said - ***"My martial arts instructor has taught me that you should never strike out of rage."***

The samurai paused and said - ***"your master seems wise, and he is correct."***

His anger eased, and they were able to reach a deal that the fisherman would pay back the amount in a year.

Here comes the actual learning from this story

When the samurai got home, still shaking from what had occurred to the fisherman, he noticed light emanating from his room. It was strange. It was already past midnight.

Slowly and carefully, he approached the bed and found his wife sleeping. He noticed someone sleeping next to her too. He got closer and noticed it was another samurai.

He instantly pulled out his sword. He crept cautiously to the bed, about to do something foolish, but suddenly he remembered the fisherman's words - ***"you should never strike out of rage."***

Then he took a deep breath, crept out of the room, and simply shouted, "I'm here!"

His wife cheerfully greeted him. The samurai's mother followed behind her out of the room. "Look who's arrived!" exclaimed his wife. She was afraid of being alone at home, so she asked her mother-in-law to keep her company. The samurai's mother had dressed like a samurai in case a robber broke in. If a robber spotted her, he would mistake her for a samurai and leave them alone.

A year later, the story of the samurai and the fisherman concluded. The samurai returned to the fisherman's village. The fisherman was expecting him. He had the money and interest because he had had a good year.

The samurai embraced him. "Keep that money," he urged. ***"You owe nothing to me. I'm the one who owes you."***

This simple story explains to us the importance of pausing before taking action.

It is preferable to pause the conversation or circumstance than to act in a way you will later regret. Taking a step back allows you to process your feelings and consider them before reacting.

In our daily life, we face so many situations that trigger our emotions to come out immediately. For example, your coworker sent you a passive-aggressive email, which you want to address in person. Perhaps you need to provide some harsh comments to a coworker. Maybe you've chosen to talk to your manager about some rising friction on your team.

You may have also faced similar issues with your partner in your relationships.

When you've decided to talk about a problem with a coworker or partner, it's tempting to start the conversation immediately.

Isn't there no better moment than the present? No, not quite.

When discussing a conflict, emotions frequently run high, and going into the conversation unprepared may lead to an ineffective, confrontational debate. You may spoil your relationships, lose clients, job or even ruin your career if you go with the immediate flow of your emotional state.

Taking the time to mentally prepare can help you stay calm, increase the likelihood that the conversation will go smoothly, and improve the final result. Becoming emotionally prepared is likely the most important job you should do before taking further action.

MENTAL PREPAREDNESS

Despite how challenging people may be, they are not the most significant barrier to saying NO effectively.

Actually, **WE** are the problem!

It is a human tendency that we are inclined to reactive behavior than a proactive one. **We often act with strong feelings but unclear motives**. We act when we're angry. Fear causes us to escape. We need to become proactive, forward-thinking, and purposeful if we want to say NO effectively.

1) Examine your mindset and plan to frame your conversation positively: If you're preparing for a "tough" discussion, you may be feeling apprehensive, stressed, furious, or disturbed about it ahead of time. To reduce these negative emotions, consider it a regular discussion and frame it positively.

For example, instead of discussing a negative performance review about your team, you may have a positive discussion regarding progress. Similarly, propose an alternative solution instead of saying NO to your boss.

You can apply the same rule during tough conversations with your life partner, colleague, boss, etc. Such positively constructed talks are more effective and can save your relationship with the other person. There's no sugarcoating here. **Be realistic about the difficulty of the discussion, but try to frame it positively.** You might convince yourself: *"The other person and I have always respected each other, and even though we may have to tackle uncomfortable issues, we'll work through them together."*

Keep your attention on what you are likely to benefit from the discussion. **Jeff Weiss,** *a partner at Boston-based Vantage Partners and author of the HBR Guide to Negotiating,* advises, **"Presume you have something to learn; assume there is a more creative solution than you've thought of."**

Regardless of the other person's view, you have a better chance of finding common ground if you approach the conversation with an open mind.

2) Put yourself in the other person's shoes: Instead of standing at your viewpoint only, consider the matter from your opponent's point of view also. Consider what your coworker or partner might be experiencing.

Even though you disagree with it, they have a reason for acting the way they have so far. Assume you are in his/her position - *"What would I do if I were in her shoes,"* for example? *"What if I were the one receiving the report? What if I was my boss instead?"*

Also, consider - what the other person is trying to accomplish. If you want to solve it, you'll need to understand what their objectives are. Find the points where you and the other person agree on the topics. You may build on this mutual understanding to address problems together.

If you're confused, ask someone what they believe is going on in your opponent's thoughts. Say something like, *"I'd love to offer some coaching and advice. Although I haven't had much experience with John, I know you have. Could you perhaps explain how he would view this scenario?"*

Be as clear and transparent as you can in asking others. Focus on the real issues rather than simply gaining sympathy, and then you can expect to get honest feedback from them.

This is also an excellent practice to **make a list of concerns you want to address** with your counterpart before you meet. This will make it easier for you to demonstrate that you care about their viewpoint enough to give it some thought in advance and learn more about how they see the problem once you are face to face.

3) Express your emotions: In the **Harvard Business Review** article **Emotional Agility**, psychologist **Susan David** writes, *"Suppressing your emotions - deciding not to say something when you're upset - can lead to terrible results."*

She says, *"They'll probably manifest themselves in other ways if you don't express your emotions."*

These are known as **"Emotional Leaks"** in psychology.

Have you ever yelled at your partner or child after a difficult day at work - an issue that wasn't their fault?

When you suppress your emotions, you're more inclined to use sarcasm or inappropriate language to express yourself instead.

Suppressing your feelings has physical costs (including cardiovascular health issues) and adverse effects on your memory, relationships, and other areas of your life.

By expressing your feelings beforehand, you can stop your emotions from leaking out during the conversation or at home. You'll be more composed and controlled when you vent out your feelings and have discussions at the right time.

There is a significant payback even if it takes 10 minutes to have the conversation. You'll enter the conversation with the correct frame of mind, confidence, and a clear idea of what you want to accomplish. And once you exit the discussion, you will be more relaxed, calm, and satisfied.

ACCEPTING WHY IT'S OK TO SAY NO

"Making the right decision late is always preferable to acting upon the wrong one merely because you feel you should."

- Ravi Lalit Tewari

There is a proverb - ***Saying YES when we should be saying NO is the cause of half of today's issues.***

In this fast-moving life, we frequently experience intense pressure to perform actions we do not want to. We put this pressure on ourselves rather often. We constantly think about what we should do, what people expect from us, how we should fulfill the need of our clients, how to save our relationships, or even how to look genuine in front of others.

These kinds of thoughts actually have the power to paralyze us, overwhelm us, and leave us feeling conflicted, constrained, or anxious. And then we tend to neglect the value of saying NO.

Whether we say YES or NO, life continues to flow, move, and advance. We definitely have the option of how we want to move ahead. **The secret to leading a fulfilling life is discovering a way to balance courtesy and kindness without compromising our feelings of self-worth**.

There will always be requests from people. You'll sometimes be able to help; other times, you won't.

Believe me, you are still a nice man!

PRIORITIZING NEEDS & FEELINGS

After all, it would be best if you prioritized your needs and feelings because you are the most significant person in your life. You deserve it!

When your needs conflict with those of someone you care about, it can feel challenging. While putting your needs ahead of others may seem selfish, it can be **a profound act of self-care** and emphasizes the value of learning to say NO.

You will run out of energy if you prioritize everyone else's needs before your own.

Establish boundaries to support your emotions, and learn to accept that you cannot always influence other people's opinions.

Do not hold the belief that you are unable to say NO because:

- Others will see you with hate
- You'll probably offend your colleagues
- You feel guilty and worried that others may stop liking you

If you realize you weren't being true to yourself, it's alright to say NO even after you've already said YES. **Making the right decision late is always preferable to acting upon the wrong one merely because you feel you should**.

I have got the below reasons for you to understand why it's OK to say NO:

#1) If you aren't taking care of yourself, you cannot take care of others too

It could be challenging for you to think of ways to say NO if you are someone who is really skilled at taking care of people. You're accustomed to considering other people and ensuring that everyone is alright. You give the people in your life a wonderful gift when you do this.

You must, however, ensure that your needs are satisfied to continue providing that loving care to other people. **The key to self-care is developing the ability to say NO.** You may continue caring for others while maintaining your physical and emotional well-being by establishing healthy boundaries.

#2) You'll never be able to influence how people perceive you

Whatever you do or say, people will either assess you favorably or unfavorably. Don't worry about this trivial issue. **Make sure it doesn't ruin your day**.

Stop making decisions about whether to answer YES or NO based on your concern about what other people may think.

#3) NO is a respectable way to respond

If you agree to something when you genuinely don't want to, it could cause resentment and damage the relationship. When you say NO when you mean it, you are demonstrating respect for both yourself and the other person.

Because you're being sincere and genuine, which are traits that foster good relationships. Saying NO has the added benefit of setting an example for those in your life. This could serve as a good illustration of how crucial this idea is. You might encourage them to establish good boundaries with you or others in the future and enhance your connections with them.

#4) Every time you say NO to something, you are also saying YES to something else

You just said YES to spending your time on something you prefer when you politely declined to attend something that would have required time. This can involve getting more rest, exercising, watching Netflix, or spending time with close friends and family.

#5) The decisions you make in your life are going to have the most impact on you

You will be most impacted by your decisions, although many choose to ignore this reality.

- *You will be the person under the most stress if you make a decision but don't follow through*
- *You will be the one with a terrible hangover and a ton of customer complaints the next day if you agree to a crazy party at eleven at night.*

You will suffer significantly in the long term if you agree to a lifetime commitment that you are not truly satisfied with!

#6) Only you have the genuine ability to determine your priorities in life

Can anybody in your life decide the priorities of your life? Can anybody choose how and when you should feel happy and contented?

Your life's decisions will determine how happy you are.

Say NO if you are unsure of anything.

Say NO if you're hesitating because you know you're not very excited about the proposal.

Say NO if it's not actually what you desire.

Nobody has the authority to instruct you on the specific things you need to engage in to feel content

and pleased in life. The only person who can accomplish this for themselves is you!

#7) Life doesn't stop when you say NO

Life keeps moving forward no matter what you say or don't say.

Because you always say YES, you can spend the rest of your life rushing, moving quickly, and running about.

Or you might choose to live a life of leisure, taking things slowly and relishing each moment by refusing to do the things that don't truly matter.

It's up to you. Lead the life you desire! Create your own fate. **If you understand that it's acceptable to say NO, you are on your way to creating your destiny**.

This is your life. So, make decisions that will benefit you and your well-being. If doing so requires your NO, then do so openly. Because **when you say NO to the conditions you do not want in your life, you are indirectly saying YES to yourself and the important things in your life - which is undoubtedly an excellent thing!**

Saying NO and drawing limits will become more natural as you practice. If you are thinking about how to begin, here you go - **practice low-risk situations, such as rejecting something a salesperson is offering**.

As your confidence and comfort levels increase, you can easily say NO in the circumstances with more significant stakes. For instance, you might refuse to help a loved one when they ask you to because you don't feel capable of doing so.

It's natural to want to immediately say YES to please the people in our lives, but it's crucial to resist this urge. Instead, we must learn to take a breath, check in with ourselves, and observe what we truly want. If we acknowledge that we really do mean YES, then our decision to say YES is genuine.

It's great to have the ability to say that we genuinely mean NO. **Regularly using specific techniques to help us say NO may improve our relationships and become more sincere, genuine, and resentment-free**.

In our future lessons, we will learn and practice such methods and techniques in detail. So, keep reading and keep learning...

3

The Role of Limiting Beliefs in Saying NO

Your beliefs become your thoughts, Your thoughts become your words, Your words become your actions, Your actions become your habits, Your habits become your values, and Your values become your destiny.

- Mahatma Gandhi

THE STORY

Once upon a time, in a far-off land, there was an elephant trainer who had a young elephant under his care. The trainer knew the key to keeping the elephant in captivity was to teach it not to escape. So, when the elephant was still just a baby, the trainer chained its leg to a huge log. Every time the elephant tried to escape, the log proved stronger, and the elephant eventually gave up.

As the elephant grew bigger and stronger, it became so used to its captivity that it no longer even attempted to escape. Even when the trainer would tie the chain around the elephant's leg to something as small as a tiny twig, the elephant wouldn't even try to break free. The elephant, now huge and strong, was nevertheless tied to its past since it had grown accustomed to captivity.

This elephant and its twig were not so different from you and the limitations imposed on you by your childhood.

ROLE OF LIMITING BELIEFS

Negative self-talk or self-imposed restrictions are examples of limiting beliefs that can keep you from acting in particular circumstances. Limiting beliefs can make you doubt your capacity to assert yourself or fear the repercussions of doing so, which is one way you can keep yourself from saying NO.

For example, a person with a limiting belief that they are not good at setting boundaries may be reluctant to say NO to a request from a coworker or friend, even if they do not want to do what is asked of them. They may fear that saying NO will cause the other person to think less of them or lead to conflict.

Similarly, a person with a limiting belief that they are not important or valuable may be more likely to say YES to requests, even if they do not want to do them, to please others and gain their approval. They may feel that they are not worthy of asserting themselves and that their needs are not as important as those of others.

Negative thoughts can lower team spirit and productivity when it comes to limiting beliefs at work. Imagine you are developing a new strategy but lack the self-confidence to suggest a more effective alternative. There is no doubt that the result won't be innovative.

Here are some examples of limiting beliefs that can hold you back:

- I am not good enough
- I am not smart enough
- I am not worthy of love
- I am not capable of achieving my goals
- I am not strong enough to handle stress
- I am not attractive enough
- I am not successful enough
- I will never be able to change
- I don't deserve to be happy
- I am not important
- I am not in control of my life
- I am not capable of making my own decisions
- I am not good at making friends
- I am not meant to be successful
- I am not qualified enough to do that

Saying NO can be difficult because of limiting beliefs in several ways:

1. **Self-doubt and Fear of Rejection**

Limiting beliefs can make it difficult for you to say NO by causing self-doubt and fear of rejection. These beliefs can cause you to doubt your ability to assert yourself and set boundaries.

You may believe that you are not worthy of standing up for yourself and your needs, making you feel that your needs are not as important as those of others.

Additionally, you may worry that others will reject you, ridicule you, or be disappointed in you, leading to the fear of rejection. This fear can make it difficult for you to say NO, causing you to keep saying YES to everything that comes your way.

2. Fear of Conflict

Limiting beliefs can also cause individuals to fear conflict. They may believe that saying NO or expressing their opinions will lead to an argument or confrontation. As a result, they may avoid expressing their thoughts or feelings or give in to others' demands to avoid conflict.

It can be problematic if you have this kind of limiting belief that always makes you afraid of conflict. Because it can prevent you from standing up for yourself and asserting your needs and wants. It can also lead to resentment and passive-aggressive behavior.

3. Low Self-esteem

Limiting beliefs can cause you to have low self-esteem in several ways. These beliefs can shape how you see yourself, your abilities, and your worth.

Some examples of how limiting beliefs can contribute to low self-esteem include:

- **Believing that one is not good enough:** An individual who thinks they are not good enough may compare themselves unfavorably to others and may feel that they are not worthy of love, success, or happiness. This can lead to feelings of inadequacy and low self-worth.

- **Believing that one is incapable:** An individual who believes they are incapable of achieving specific goals or not intelligent or talented enough may feel discouraged and defeated. This can lead to a lack of motivation and a lack of confidence in one's own abilities.

- **Believing that one is not deserving:** An individual who holds the belief that they are not deserving of good things may feel guilty or ashamed when they experience success or happiness. This can lead to feelings of unworthiness and low self-esteem.

Low self-esteem can make it difficult for you to say NO because you may lack confidence in yourself and your abilities, feel a strong need for validation, or feel guilty for standing up for yourself. This can lead to a tendency to conform to others' wishes and avoid asserting yourself.

LIMITING BELIEFS ARE CHANGING YOUR LIFE AS A WHOLE

Let's assume that you think everyone is out to take advantage of you. You will perceive all of your encounters through the lens of that mindset. Due to the ***human brain's wiring***, you will always seek and discover evidence to support this belief.

But let's do the opposite. Let's assume that you genuinely think people are friendly, helpful, and generally willing to help you. The lens through which you see your interactions and relationships will then be determined by this belief. Your brain will continually search for and gather proof to back up this notion. This is the kind of reality that you will typically encounter.

The people you interact with might not differ depending on your beliefs. But how you understand their behaviors will change. Your brain will give the same behavior a different meaning depending on your beliefs.

Beliefs are analogous to a piece of computer code that instructs your mind to process information in a particular way.

This is just one simple illustration of how a single belief may significantly impact how you live your life. Think about the fact that you have hundreds or perhaps thousands of beliefs contributing to how you perceive the world!

HOW LIMITING BELIEFS ARE FORMED

Forming limiting beliefs is a complex process that can be influenced by various factors.

As is to be expected, most limiting beliefs are formed when we are young and still developing our identities and worldviews. Therefore, each person will likely have a unique set of limiting beliefs.

However, limiting beliefs generally come from a few different places, such as:

1. **Your education and how you were raised**

How you were raised, the beliefs instilled in you by your family, and how you personally interpret those beliefs can significantly impact how you view yourself and the world around you. This can include various topics, from feelings of self-worth and validation to career aspirations and social interactions.

Additionally, the education and perspectives provided by not only formal education but also by family, friends, and peers during your upbringing can shape your beliefs about your abilities and the world.

These experiences and perspectives **shape your own understanding of what you are capable of and what you cannot do**.

2. **From various life experiences**

Life experiences, especially those that end negatively, can play a significant role in forming limiting beliefs. Negative experiences such as failure, rejection, or trauma can lead to the development of limiting beliefs about oneself and the world.

For example, if you have ever experienced failure in a relationship, you may develop the belief that ***you are not worthy of love or that you are not capable of maintaining a healthy relationship***.

Similarly, if you have ever experienced rejection in a job interview, you may develop the belief that ***you are not qualified or capable of achieving your career aspirations***.

Traumatic experiences can also lead to the development of limiting beliefs.

For example, if you have ever been through a traumatic event such as a natural disaster, accident, or abuse, you may develop the belief that ***the world is dangerous or that you are weak or not strong enough***.

3. Through the process of socialization

One way in which limiting beliefs are formed is through the process of socialization.

From a young age, we are exposed to various messages and beliefs from our family, friends, and society at large. These messages can shape our perceptions and beliefs about ourselves and our world.

For example, an individual repeatedly told that they are not good enough may internalize this belief, leading to feelings of inadequacy and low self-worth.

4. **Through past experiences and traumas**

Another way in which limiting beliefs are formed is through past experiences and traumas. Negative experiences such as abuse, neglect, or rejection can lead to the development of limiting beliefs.

For example, an individual who has been through an abusive relationship may believe they are not worthy of love or respect.

5. **Through cognitive distortions**

Additionally, limiting beliefs can also be formed through cognitive distortions, which are patterns of thinking that lead to inaccurate or irrational beliefs.

For example, black-and-white thinking, personalization, and catastrophizing.

STRATEGIES FOR IDENTIFYING LIMITING BELIEFS

As we learned that limiting beliefs can be like a cozy blanket that keeps us snuggled in our comfort zone. But they can also hold us back from reaching our full potential and achieving our goals, both in our personal and professional lives.

Regardless of our level of awareness, these thoughts can appear firmly entrenched. But the good news is we can change these negative thoughts that keep us from reaching our goals! By shifting our thinking, we can open up a whole new world of possibilities.

It is important to note that simply verbalizing the belief that "People are kind" will not automatically result in individuals exhibiting kindness. This type of thinking is called **"wishful thinking"** rather than a **"genuine belief."**

A belief is formed when one's perspective changes, resulting in a shift in neural connections within the brain. This phenomenon is referred to as a "Mindset Shift."

There may be hundreds of self-limiting beliefs are there within us. Knowingly or unknowingly, those are affecting us every day in our life. So, the crucial point here is how we identify our limiting beliefs.

I have compiled **a list of 6 activities** that have been helping hundreds of my clients identify their limiting beliefs. I hope these will be helpful for you as well. These are as follows:

1. Journaling

Journaling is a great way to identify and work through limiting beliefs. When you journal, you can write down your thoughts and feelings in a private and safe space, which can help you better understand them.

One way to use journaling to identify limiting beliefs is to set aside some time each day to write about any negative thoughts or feelings that come up. As you write, you may start to notice patterns in your thoughts and feelings. These patterns can be a clue to underlying limiting beliefs. For example, if you find yourself frequently writing about feeling inadequate or not good enough, you may have a limiting belief that you are not worthy or capable.

Another way to use journaling to identify limiting beliefs is to reflect on specific situations or experiences that have caused you to feel upset, frustrated, or stuck. As you write about these experiences, try to identify what thoughts or beliefs were present in your mind when you were feeling this way. These thoughts can often reveal limiting beliefs you may not have been aware of.

2. Self-reflection

Self-reflection is another powerful tool for identifying limiting beliefs. It involves reflecting on your thoughts, feelings, and actions to better understand yourself and your behavior. When you engage in self-reflection, you can start to identify patterns in your thoughts and behavior that may be holding you back.

One way to use self-reflection to identify limiting beliefs is to regularly take time to sit quietly with yourself and simply observe your thoughts as they come and go. As you do this, you may start to notice patterns in your thinking, such as negative self-talk or thoughts of self-doubt. These patterns can be a clue to underlying limiting beliefs.

Self-reflection can also help you identify how your limiting beliefs may impact your behavior and how you can change your behavior to challenge these limiting beliefs. It can be a powerful tool for gaining self-awareness and making positive changes in your life.

Remember that self-reflection is an ongoing process, and it takes time, be patient and compassionate with yourself.

3. **Mindfulness Practices**

Mindfulness is the practice of being fully present and engaged in the current moment while also observing one's thoughts, feelings, and physical sensations without judgment.

By consistently implementing mindfulness techniques, you can increase self-awareness and discern patterns in your thoughts, emotions, and behaviors. This heightened awareness can assist in identifying limiting beliefs that may impede personal growth and development.

One way that mindfulness practices can help identify limiting beliefs is through the practice of **"thought-watching."** This involves simply observing your thoughts as they come and go without engaging with them or getting caught up in them. As you do this, you may start to notice patterns in your thinking, such as negative self-talk or thoughts of self-doubt. These patterns can be a clue to underlying limiting beliefs.

Another way that mindfulness practices can help identify limiting beliefs is by becoming more aware of the emotions and physical sensations that arise in response to certain thoughts or situations. For example, if you notice that you feel anxious or stressed in certain situations, you can use mindfulness to explore what thoughts or beliefs may contribute to this emotional response.

I have also observed from my past experiences that mindfulness practices help identify limiting beliefs by helping you become more aware of the body's sensations, breathing, and posture. When you become more aware of your body, you can start to identify patterns of tension or discomfort related to limiting beliefs, such as feeling tightness in your chest when you think of a specific situation.

4. NLP Techniques

NLP, or **Neuro-Linguistic Programming**, is a set of techniques that can help identify limiting beliefs.

NLP is based on the idea that our thoughts, language, and behavior are interconnected and that we can change others by changing one. NLP techniques can help identify limiting beliefs by allowing us to understand the relationship between our thoughts, language, and behavior and how they influence each other.

One NLP technique that can help identify limiting beliefs is the **"Reframing"** technique, which involves looking at a situation or belief from a different perspective. This can help to reveal new insights and understandings about a belief and can also help to challenge limiting beliefs.

Another NLP technique that can help identify limiting beliefs is the **"Meta Model"** technique, which involves asking specific questions to get to the underlying meaning of a belief. This can help uncover any limiting beliefs hidden behind the surface of thought or statement.

The **"Anchoring"** technique, used to create a positive emotional state and associate it with a specific word, gesture, or situation, can also change limiting beliefs. It can be changed over time by anchoring a positive state to a limiting belief.

NLP techniques can be an effective way to identify limiting beliefs and change the way we think, feel, and behave. It's important to remember that it takes time and practice to master NLP techniques, but consistent effort can be a powerful tool to identify limiting beliefs and create positive change in your life.

KINDLY NOTE: It's also important to note that NLP is not scientifically proven, and its effectiveness may vary based on the individual and the specific technique used. It's always a good idea to consult a licensed therapist or counselor before undergoing any NLP treatment.

5. Cognitive Behavioral Therapy

Cognitive Behavioral Therapy (CBT) is a widely used psychological treatment that can help identify and change limiting beliefs. CBT is predicated on the notion that altering our thoughts can alter our feelings and actions.

One of the most common ways to identify our limiting beliefs using CBT is through **"Cognitive Restructuring,"** which is the process of questioning and challenging your thoughts to change them.

This can involve identifying any negative thoughts, such as *"I'm not good enough"* or *"I can't do this,"* and then questioning the evidence for and against those thoughts. You can change limiting beliefs by looking for counterexamples and alternative ways of thinking. You can ask the following counter questions:

- *What evidence do I have to support this thought?*
- *Is there any evidence that contradicts this thought?*
- *What would I say to a friend in this situation?*
- *How would I respond to someone else who had this thought about themselves?*

Another CBT technique is **"Behavioral Experiments,"** which involves testing thoughts by changing your behavior and observing the consequences.

This can help you to see the effects of your limiting beliefs practically and understand the relationship between your thoughts, feelings, and behavior.

For example:

Suppose you believe "I'm not good enough," and this thought leads you to avoid social situations. To test this belief, you can conduct a behavioral experiment by intentionally putting yourself in a social situation and observing your thoughts, feelings, and behaviors. For example, you could attend a party, have conversations with others, and actively participate in activities. After the event, you can reflect on your experience and compare it to your original belief. This will help you evaluate whether your belief was accurate or not.

CBT has been proven effective in helping individuals identify and change limiting beliefs and can address various mental health issues such as depression, anxiety, PTSD, and more.

6. Seeking Feedback

Our beliefs are often influenced by our past experiences and the people around us, and seeking feedback from others can help us to see our thoughts and behaviors from a different perspective.

One way to seek feedback is to ask people you trust and respect for their honest opinions about your thoughts, feelings, and behavior. For example, if you believe you are not good enough, you can ask someone you trust if they see any evidence of this in you and what examples they have that counter that belief.

Another way to seek feedback is to engage in group therapy or support groups, where you can share your thoughts and feelings with others who may have similar experiences. This can help you to see your thoughts and behaviors from a different perspective and identify any limiting beliefs that may be holding you back.

You can also get feedback from a therapist or coach, who can help you to identify limiting beliefs and provide you with different perspectives on your thoughts and behavior. They can also help you understand the underlying causes of your limiting beliefs and guide you in changing them.

STRATEGIES FOR OVERCOMING LIMITING BELIEFS

Uncovering one's own limiting beliefs can be a formidable task, yet it is the first step in overcoming them. The journey may prove difficult, but rest assured, it is not impossible.

Let me offer you my **5-step method** to set you on your way:

1. **Challenge Your Belief by Asking - *WHAT IF I'M WRONG?***

Ponder upon the limiting belief that holds you back and ask yourself, *"What if this belief is inaccurate?"* For example, if you believe that your height precludes you from finding romantic partners or that your gender bars you from career advancement, imagine a reality where these assumptions are unfounded.

Challenging your beliefs may surprise you with its ease and simplicity. By entertaining the possibility that your beliefs may be flawed, you open yourself to alternative perspectives and opportunities. More often than not, the solutions to our perceived limitations are within reach.

2. Then Ask - HOW DOES MY BELIEF BENEFIT ME?

Getting flooded with limiting beliefs?

It is natural to feel as though we are at the mercy of our limiting beliefs; however, the truth is that these beliefs often serve a purpose in our lives. Consider the elephant who believes she cannot pull away from the fence post. This belief served her in the past, protecting her from the effort and disappointment of failure. Similarly, we hold onto limiting beliefs to protect ourselves from struggle and failure or because they make us feel unique and deserving of special attention.

It's essential to understand the role they play in our lives to overcome limiting beliefs. Ask yourself, *"How is this belief serving me?"*

Consider whether the benefits of holding onto this belief outweigh the costs. Remember, beliefs only persist if they serve us in some way, so weigh the value of your belief and determine if it is truly worth holding onto.

3. Now Create Alternative Beliefs - Empowering Beliefs

Now is the time to replace your limiting beliefs with empowering ones.

This can be achieved by reframing your thoughts and adopting a more positive perspective. Instead of focusing on the negative aspects of a situation, focus on the potential opportunities and possibilities. For example, instead of thinking, *"I can't do this,"* try thinking, *"I can learn to do this."*

Adopting *affirmations* and *visualization techniques* is also beneficial.

Affirmations are positive statements that can help to create empowering beliefs by reinforcing positive thoughts and beliefs about oneself. They work by training the mind to focus on positive thoughts and ideas; by repetition, they can help change negative beliefs and thought patterns.

When you repeat affirmations, you actively replace negative thoughts with positive ones. The more you repeat an affirmation, the more it becomes ingrained in your subconscious mind, and the more likely you are to believe it and act on it.

For example, if you believe you are not good enough, you can use affirmations such as *"I am worthy and deserving of success"* or *"I am capable and competent"* to counteract that belief and reinforce a more positive belief about yourself.

You can use affirmations to set specific goals also and affirm as if you have already achieved them. For example, an affirmation like *"I am financially secure and successful. I'm already making 1 million dollars every month happily and easily"* can help to reinforce the belief that you can achieve financial stability and success.

Affirmations are like a magical key that can help you to unlock the doors of limiting beliefs and negative thoughts and open up to a world of endless possibilities.

Here are a few examples of such positive affirmations I usually work on with my clients:

- I am confident in my abilities and trust in my decisions.
- I am worthy of love and happiness.
- I am capable of achieving my goals.
- I am surrounded by abundance and prosperity.
- I am strong and capable of overcoming any challenge.
- I am grateful for the blessings in my life.
- I am a positive force in the world and make a difference.
- I am in control of my thoughts and emotions.
- I am deserving of respect and treat myself with kindness.
- I am constantly improving and growing as a person.

Visualization is another powerful tool for creating empowering beliefs because it allows you to see yourself achieving your goals and living the life you want in your mind's eye. When you visualize yourself succeeding, it can help you believe in your ability to make it happen.

It works by activating the same brain areas used when experiencing something.

When you visualize yourself in a specific situation, you create a mental image that your brain interprets as real. This can help create feelings of confidence and motivation and improve your ability to focus and concentrate.

Remember that it is essential to practice consistency and patience in the process of replacing limiting beliefs with empowering ones. Changing beliefs takes time, and it is a continuous journey. But with persistence and effort, you can break free from limiting beliefs and achieve the success and fulfillment you desire.

4. Seek Support

Overcoming limiting beliefs can be a complex and challenging process, and it's essential to have a support system in place. Surrounding yourself with positive, supportive people who can help you to stay motivated and on track is crucial.

Having people who believe in you and your capabilities can help boost your self-confidence and make the journey of overcoming limiting beliefs less daunting.

Support can come from friends, family members, mentors, or even a coach or therapist who can help you to identify and overcome your limiting beliefs. Having someone to talk to and share your progress with can help to keep you accountable and motivated.

5. Take Action

The final step in overcoming limiting beliefs is to take action.

The key is to take small, consistent steps toward your goals. Even if it's something as small as making a phone call or writing a letter, taking action can help to build momentum and increase your confidence. The more you take action, the more you will begin to see that your limiting beliefs are not true; you can achieve your goals.

This will give you a sense of accomplishment and help you recognize your progress, further motivating you to keep going.

Remember that progress is not always linear, you might stumble and fall, but the important thing is to get back up and keep going. With a positive mindset, the right tools, and a bit of determination, you can overcome any limiting beliefs and reach your full potential.

LET'S GET MOTIVATED

Let me give you a few examples of individuals who overcame their limiting beliefs and went on to become famous figures:

1. **J.K. Rowling,** the author of the Harry Potter series, faced rejection from multiple publishers before her book was finally accepted and published. She went on to become one of the most successful authors in the world,

overcoming her limiting belief that she was not a good enough writer.

2. **Michael Jordan,** considered one of the greatest basketball players of all time, was cut from his high school basketball team. He later said, *"I have missed more than 9,000 shots in my career. I have lost almost 300 games. Twenty-six times I've been trusted to take the game-winning shot and missed. I've failed over and over and over again in my life. And that is why I succeed."* He used that failure as motivation and became one of the best basketball players ever.

3. **Oprah Winfrey,** a media executive, actress, talk show host, television producer, and philanthropist, grew up in poverty and faced abuse. She went on to become one of the most successful and influential people in media, overcoming her limiting belief that she would never escape poverty or be successful.

4. **Abraham Lincoln,** the 16th President of the United States, faced many failures before becoming president. He lost eight elections, twice failed in business, and suffered a nervous breakdown. He became one of the most successful presidents in American history, overcoming his limiting belief that he could not achieve success.

5. **Stephen King,** one of the best-selling authors of all time, was rejected 30 times before his first book was accepted for publication. He went on to become a

bestselling author and overcame his limiting belief that he would never be successful as a writer.

6. **Walt Disney,** the founder of The Walt Disney Company, was fired by a newspaper editor because "he lacked imagination and had no good ideas." He went on to create one of the most successful entertainment companies in the world, overcoming his limiting belief that he was not creative or capable of success.

7. **Helen Keller,** deaf and blind, faced many challenges but became a renowned author and lecturer. She overcame her limiting belief that her disabilities would hold her back and significantly impacted the world.

So, my friend, I hope now we understand that we can unlock our true potential and achieve success by identifying and overcoming our limiting beliefs. We are now equipped with the steps we need to take to overcome any of our limiting beliefs.

Of course, we also realize that the journey of overcoming limiting beliefs is ongoing, and it's essential to continue to reflect, grow and take action.

I believe you can shape your reality and overcome any limiting beliefs by using the right tools, a positive mindset, and a support system.

What do you think now, my friend, about any of your limiting beliefs?

Are they really true and limiting you to saying NO?

Say YES to NO!!

4

The Role of Setting Boundaries in Saying NO

You teach people how to treat you by what you allow, what you stop, and what you reinforce.

- Tony Robbins

IMPORTANCE & BENEFITS

1. Importance

During my entire mentorship career, I have experienced that setting healthy boundaries is vital to building strong and fulfilling personal and professional relationships. We often fall into the trap of constantly trying to please others without considering the impact on our well-being. But by learning to say YES to what truly matters to us and NO to what doesn't, we can create a balance that benefits everyone involved.

Remember, **"good boundaries" lead to "good relationships" and a successful life**.

The inability to establish healthy boundaries is often rooted in more profound issues such as low self-worth, a desire for validation from others, learned helplessness, or a fear of rejection and criticism. These underlying emotional struggles can significantly impact one's ability to effectively set boundaries and must be addressed to foster healthy relationships.

Setting clear boundaries is crucial in fostering trust and building healthy relationships. Even if others may not agree with your decisions, they will still respect you for standing firm in your beliefs. Establishing boundaries also promotes a sense of safety and security in your relationships, as respecting one's privacy leads to feeling heard, validated, and valued.

Additionally, setting boundaries ensures that you are not taken for granted by those close to you, be it loved ones or colleagues. That's why communicating your boundaries clearly and assertively to maintain healthy and fulfilling relationships is essential.

When it comes to saying NO, setting boundaries is especially important. Here are a few reasons why:

- **Self-care:** Saying NO is often necessary for self-care, especially when faced with overwhelming or unrealistic demands. Setting boundaries allows you to prioritize your own well-being and avoid burnout.

- **Respect:** Setting boundaries is a way of showing respect for oneself and one's needs and wants. It communicates that you value yourself and your time and are unwilling to compromise on your priorities.

- **Clarity:** Setting boundaries provides clarity in relationships. It helps to establish what is and is not acceptable behavior and what you are willing to tolerate or compromise on. This can prevent misunderstandings and conflicts in the future.

- **Empowerment:** Setting boundaries is an act of self-empowerment. It allows individuals to take control of their lives and make choices that align with their values and goals.

- **Relationship building:** Setting boundaries can also improve relationships. It allows for open and honest communication and helps to establish mutual respect and trust. It is important to remember that while it is important to consider the needs of others, it is equally important to prioritize and advocate for your own needs. Setting and maintaining healthy boundaries is crucial in preventing verbal, emotional, or physical abuse. It is wise to recognize that those who cannot accept and respect the changes in your identity may not be the right people for you to have in your life. It is advisable to prioritize self-care and surround yourself with individuals who support and respect your boundaries.

So, you can understand that boundaries are the guidelines for how others should treat you, what behaviors are acceptable to you, and what you are willing to accept. They are based on your needs and wants, and it is not selfish to set them. Rather, it is a way of understanding your own value, setting priorities, and ensuring that others respect them. Setting boundaries allows you to create the space and time necessary to pursue your career goals and life aspirations.

2. Benefits

Establishing healthy boundaries is a fundamental aspect of self-care and self-respect and should serve as the foundation of your personal leadership.

Assertiveness, without the need for aggression, is key in this process. You can assert your uniqueness and core values by defining and enforcing healthy boundaries.

The ability to assertively decline new commitments demonstrates your respect for those already made. Boundaries are not simply about obtaining personal desires; instead, they allow you to live according to your terms and conditions.

There are several benefits of implementing healthy boundaries in both personal and professional spheres, including:

- The ability to actively listen and consider alternative perspectives while respecting your own.
- The practice of self-respect through the assertion of your own beliefs and values.
- The prevention of potential conflicts & resentment.
- The imposition of reasonable consequences for any violation of established boundaries.

- The ability to prioritize your own needs and well-being.
- Better communication and understanding in relationships. For example, setting a boundary to not accept phone calls after 9 pm can help improve communication in a romantic relationship.
- The development of the skills to make better choices in your life. And preventing you from taking on too much or making commitments you can't fulfill.
- **Prioritizing your time and energy:** Saying NO to specific commitments and requests can help you focus on the things that are most important to you, whether that's your work, your family, your health, or something else. When you set clear boundaries, you can prioritize your time and energy on the things that matter most to you and that you are most passionate about.

Similarly, if we look into various areas of life, setting boundaries can benefit us in several ways, including:

- **Personal relationships:** Setting boundaries in personal relationships can help you communicate your needs and wants clearly, establish trust and respect, and create a more balanced and healthy dynamic with others. It can also help you avoid feeling taken advantage of or resentful towards others.
- **Workplace:** Setting boundaries in the workplace can help you manage your time and energy more effectively, avoid burnout, and maintain a healthy

work-life balance. It can also help you establish clear expectations with colleagues and managers and avoid feeling overwhelmed by unrealistic demands or expectations.

- **Physical and emotional health:** Setting boundaries can help you take better care of your physical and emotional health. It can help you make time for self-care and prioritize your physical and mental well-being, improving your overall quality of life.
- **Finances:** Setting boundaries with your finances can help you establish a budget and stick to it, avoid overspending and accumulating debt, and achieve your financial goals.
- **Digital life:** Setting boundaries with technology and social media can help you manage your time and reduce distractions and over-connectivity; it can also help you avoid adverse effects on mental health like anxiety and depression.
- **Spirituality:** Setting boundaries in your spiritual life can help you establish a regular practice, avoid feeling overwhelmed by religious or spiritual obligations, and maintain a deeper connection with your beliefs and values.

And here are a few lines for you. I hope you'll like them:

Saying NO with boundaries set,

Allows for clarity, respect, and time to rest.

Prioritizing self, avoiding burnout,

A reputation for reliability, values upheld, without a doubt.

So let us learn to set them well,

To live our lives with balance and a healthy dwell.

BOUNDARY SETTING - THE 5-STEP FORMULA

As we saw above, setting boundaries and effectively communicating them is crucial because it helps establish healthy relationships with others, promotes self-awareness and self-respect, and allows us to take control of our own lives and well-being.

We also learned that setting boundaries helps us care for our physical, emotional, and mental health. It allows us to set limits on behavior that is harmful or not beneficial for ourselves.

Effective communication is vital when it comes to setting and maintaining healthy boundaries. The more precisely and clearly you express your limits, the more likely you will be respected by others. While it may take some repetition, it is important to stand firm in your boundaries and not feel the need to apologize or justify them.

The 5-Step Formula

Now the obvious question arises - **How to set those boundaries and communicate them effectively?**

The key to establishing limits is communication. Sharing your needs and desires is the most critical step toward identifying your limitations and leading a more liberated life.

Step#1) Clarify and articulate your Boundaries

Concretizing your boundaries is the initial and most crucial step in setting them. Because they seem unseen to us in our daily lives, boundaries are frequently ambiguous and vague.

However, you may gain much more clarity about where you want to establish a boundary between yourself and others by envisioning your limits and writing them down. Take a moment to consider your life's current status and ask:

- What is making me uncomfortable or stressed out needlessly?
- What do I like versus what do I hate daily basis?
- What or who provides me with energy?
- What aspects of my life do I find draining?
- What gives me a sense of security, acceptance, and worth?

On a blank sheet of paper, draw a big circle. Write everything that helps you feel secure and at ease inside the circle.

You can consider the below examples:

- Your regular routine
- Positive remarks from your spouse
- Love and hugs from your family

- Leaving your work-related stress at work
- Your loved ones should communicate clearly with you
- Freedom to choose how you want to spend your leisure time

Next, write down anything and everything that makes you uncomfortable, hurts, irritates, or makes you feel emotionally spent on the outside of the circle. These are the individuals or circumstances that are straining your boundaries.

For example:

- Your parents dictating your course of action in life
- Working on assignments after hours rather than putting self-care first
- Being concerned with what others may think of you
- Your close buddy requests a loan of money
- At lunch, your coworker continually complains about her personal issues

- Your roommate taking your food from the refrigerator
- Your partner or girlfriend is in charge of your conversations and social interactions
- Strange bar patrons approaching or touching you without your permission
- Your relatives inquire deeply or privately about your life

Your boundaries are physically manifested in this circle. It's time to examine anything outside the circle and see if a limit can be established to prevent or resolve those concerns in the future.

Step #2) State your boundaries clearly

You occasionally believe that people should be aware of your boundaries. But how would they know when they've crossed the boundary if you didn't make it obvious where you drew the line?

Setting boundaries in your head without communicating them to the people in your life is among the worst mistakes you make.

This may seem complicated and frightening, but it may feel incredibly relieving once you've finished.

I remember a famous quote from **Brene Brown**, *a social psychology researcher,* ***"clear is kind, unclear is unkind!"***

You must express your boundaries once you are aware of them!

Calmly and confidently communicate your needs respectfully and straightforwardly by taking a deep breath and mustering your determination.

Let me give you a few examples of how you can clearly communicate your boundaries regarding various different areas in life:

- **When you don't have enough time:** "I can only remain for an hour" or "Please inform me if you're likely to be late."
- **When you are lacking energy:** "I'm sorry, but I cannot spare the energy to assist you with [their request] at this time, but perhaps [this resource] can."
- **When you are emotionally weak:** "I know you're struggling, and I want to support you, but right now, I don't have the emotional stamina to listen."

- **When you feel uncomfortable or need personal space:** "I find it unsettling when you [engage in an activity or touch]. I'll have to exit if you don't respect my personal space."
- **When you don't want to comment on something:** "This is not a subject I'm willing to talk about at this time."
- **When you do not agree with someone:** "Please don't impose your idea on me; I realize that we have different points of view."
- **When you don't want to post something on social media:** "I don't think it's okay for me to publish that on Instagram."

Fortunately, most individuals will respect your boundaries if notified of them and apologize if they unintentionally breach them. Without explicit communication, the boundaries become blurred. Getting burned out, being taken advantage of, or even ignoring your needs can easily lead you to more dangerous ground.

It will be simpler to maintain your boundaries if you clearly and forcefully articulate them. It is considerably simpler to respect them when they are made visible to all parties.

Step #3) Reaffirm and uphold your boundaries

Reaffirming and upholding your boundaries is important because it helps establish and maintain healthy relationships with others.

By reaffirming your boundaries, you clearly communicate your needs and expectations to others. This can prevent misunderstandings and conflicts, as people will better understand what is and is not acceptable in your relationship.

Additionally, it can also help to establish trust, as people will know that you are assertive in standing up for yourself and your needs.

There are several ways to reaffirm your boundaries:

1. **The clarity in communication:** People in your life should know exactly where your boundaries are. Use "I" statements to describe your needs and feelings, such as "I need" or "I feel." When communicating your boundaries, be firm yet respectful.

2. **Be consistent:** It's crucial to consistently enforce any boundaries you set. People will respect your boundaries more if you consistently communicate them to them.

3. **Use positive self-talk:** Practice positive self-talk and remind yourself that it is okay to set boundaries and take care of yourself. This can help to boost your confidence in enforcing your boundaries.

4. **Don't make exceptions:** It's important to stick to your boundaries, even if it may be uncomfortable or difficult to do so. Allowing exceptions can send mixed signals and undermine the importance of your boundaries.

Similarly, upholding your boundaries is also essential because it helps you take responsibility for your well-being. When you allow others to cross your limits, you may put your needs and wants aside to please them. This can lead to feelings of resentment and a loss of self-respect.

By upholding your boundaries, you prioritize your well-being and show respect for yourself.

Here are several ways to uphold your boundaries:

1. **Follow through on consequences:** If you have set consequences for someone who has repeatedly violated your boundaries, it is important to follow through on them. This could include ending a relationship or limiting contact with that person.

2. **Be assertive:** Speak up when someone is crossing your boundaries. Being assertive helps to convey that your boundaries are important and should be respected. Use "I" statements to clearly communicate your feelings and needs.

3. **Please stick to your guns:** It can be easy to cave in when someone pressures you to change your boundaries. It's important to stay firm and remember that your boundaries are in place to protect you. Don't change your boundaries to accommodate someone else's comfort. You probably don't want to convey the idea that *"occasionally it's OK for you to contact me late at night"* if you previously stated, *"I don't feel comfortable with you contacting me regarding work after hours."* Even

though it could feel unpleasant or uneasy at first, a person who genuinely wants to be in your life will respect your choice.

4. **Be willing to walk away:** If someone repeatedly violates your boundaries and refuses to respect them, be prepared to leave the relationship. This cannot be easy, but it may be necessary for your well-being.

5. **Practice self-care:** Taking care of yourself is essential for upholding your boundaries. This can include getting enough sleep, eating well, and engaging in activities that bring you joy and relaxation.

6. **Reflect on your actions:** Reflect on your activities and evaluate if you have been holding on to your boundaries. This will help you identify behavior patterns that may undermine your boundaries and make necessary adjustments.

Step #4) Don't hesitate to express your refusal

When someone asks you to do something that goes against your limits or principles, you shouldn't be scared to say NO. Forcing your limits and taking care of yourself requires using aggressive and respectful rejection language.

Saying NO can be challenging, particularly if you have a tendency to prioritize the needs of others over your own. It's crucial to remember that you have the authority to establish your own boundaries and make choices that are consistent with your needs and ideals.

Although it might be challenging, saying NO can empower and give you more control over your life.

It's crucial to utilize "I" phrases when expressing your rejection to convey your interests and sentiments, such as *"I'm sorry, I can't do that"* or *"I don't feel comfortable with it."* This makes it more apparent that your refusal is based on your own wants and ideals rather than making a personal attack on the other person.

It's imperative to be ready for any unexpected responses and outcomes that might follow your refusal. While some individuals might appreciate and understand your boundaries, others might be upset or angry. Be prepared to be empathic and considerate of the other person's sentiments while remaining adamant in your refusal.

Always remember that every YES and NO affects your reality. Healthy limits require the ability to say NO. You have the authority to decide how to use your time, energy, and resources. You probably shouldn't do it if it doesn't seem right in your heart.

It is possible to say NO without being impolite, and there is no need to explain or apologize. Be aware of situations where you mean NO when you say, *"I'm sorry, I can't,"* or *"maybe, let me get back to you."* Instead of being vague, try to clearly set boundaries to benefit all parties involved.

Step #5) Take a break for yourself

Effective boundary establishing and communication depends on practicing self-care. By making time for yourselves, you can better understand what is important to you and what boundaries must be created to safeguard your physical, emotional, and mental well-being. You are better equipped to recognize your needs and give them the attention they deserve when you take the time to look for yourself.

Taking time for yourself can also significantly affect your emotional state and capacity for assertive communication. You are more likely to feel confident and assertive while communicating your boundaries when reenergized and focused. You may concentrate and rejuvenate when you take time for yourself, which enables you to express your desires in a definite and solid way.

Self-awareness and self-control are also crucial components when effectively defining and communicating boundaries. When you take the time to look for yourself, you can develop these abilities, enabling you to react to boundary violations or requests that you cannot fulfill in a manner that is composed, precise, and aggressive rather than one that is vague or apologetic.

EXERCISE FOR YOU

Finally, towards the end, here is a small yet powerful exercise for you. Please complete this before moving to the next learning.

1. Reflect on a situation in your life where you struggled to set a boundary or communicate effectively.

2. Please write down the specific scenario, the emotions you felt, and the words you used (or wish you had used).
3. Brainstorm alternative ways you could have set a boundary or communicated more effectively in that situation.

As you continue to navigate life, it is essential to keep working on setting boundaries and communicating effectively. Remember that this is an ongoing process that requires continuing reflection and refinement. I encourage you to practice the techniques and skills you have learned in this chapter for situations that you may encounter in the future.

5

The Role of Confidence & Self-Esteem in Saying NO

Confidence comes not from always being right but from not fearing to be wrong.

- Peter T. Mcintyre

THE STORY

"Ratatouille" is a 2007 American computer-animated comedy film produced by **Pixar Animation Studios** and directed by **Brad Bird**. The story is about a rat named Remy, who lives in the sewers of Paris and dreams of becoming a chef. Despite his family's insistence that rats should stick to scavenging for scraps, Remy is determined to pursue his passion for cooking.

One day, Remy finds himself accidentally separated from his family and ends up in the kitchen of a famous Parisian restaurant, Gusteau's. There, he discovers that the restaurant's current chef, Skinner, is planning to ruin the legacy of the late Auguste Gusteau by introducing a line of frozen foods. Remy decides to help the restaurant's garbage boy, Linguini, the rightful heir of Gusteau's, become a great chef and save the restaurant.

Remy uses his sense of smell and taste to guide Linguini in the kitchen, controlling his movements by pulling on his hair. They create a dish that becomes an instant hit with the diners, and Linguini is promoted to head chef. However, their secret is soon discovered, and Linguini is fired. Remy and Linguini then open their own restaurant, which becomes a huge success.

Throughout the movie, Remy faces many obstacles, including the prejudice of humans against rats, the challenges of working in a professional kitchen, and the competition from other chefs. However, he never loses faith in himself and his abilities and ultimately proves that a rat can be a great chef.

The movie shows the **importance of self-confidence, determination, and hard work in achieving one's goals.** It also emphasizes the value of embracing one's unique talents and abilities and using them to overcome obstacles and succeed.

Now, let's talk about the real problems we face daily due to a lack of self-confidence and determination.

THE PROBLEM

1. A co-worker constantly asks to borrow small amounts of money, but you are uncomfortable with lending money and feel guilty saying NO. You lack the self-confidence to assert yourself and set boundaries, so you continue to lend money even though it causes your financial strain.

2. You are asked to take on additional responsibilities at work, but you are already overwhelmed with your current workload. You lack the self-esteem to believe that you can handle the additional tasks, and you fear that saying NO will lead to disappointment from your employer or colleagues.

3. Your friend invites you to a social event, but you are introverted and prefer to spend time alone. You lack the self-confidence to assert your preferences and say NO to the invitations, so you feel drained and resentful after going out.

4. One of your family members frequently asks favors, but you feel used and resentful. You lack the self-esteem to recognize your value and set boundaries, so you continue to do the favors even though it makes you unhappy.

5. You are asked to take on a leadership role in a community organization, but you lack the self-confidence to believe in your abilities and, at the same time, cannot say NO to the request. You feel pressure to take on the role even though it is not something you are comfortable with.

6. You are in a romantic relationship with someone emotionally manipulative, but you lack the self-esteem to recognize your worth and assert yourself. You fear that saying NO will lead to rejection or disappointment and continue to put up with the manipulation.

7. You are asked to take on a project at work that you don't have the skills or experience to handle, but you lack the self-confidence to decline the request. You fear that saying NO will lead to disappointment from their employer or colleagues.

From the above problem list, you can get an idea that a lack of self-confidence and self-esteem can lead to a variety of problems, including:

- Creating and accomplishing goals can be challenging
- Relationship establishment and maintenance challenges
- Having trouble expressing yourself and arriving at decisions
- Difficulty doing new things and taking risks
- Difficulty coping with rejection or criticism
- Difficulty believing you deserve or are worthy of nice things
- Inability to feel at ease in social circumstances
- Inability to feel positive about yourself
- Having trouble handling stress and adversity
- Difficulty succeeding in different aspects of life
- Difficulty with your physical and mental well-being

THE SOLUTION

WHAT IS SELF-CONFIDENCE?

Self-confidence is your belief in your abilities, qualities, and judgments. It is the level of trust and confidence you have in yourself, your abilities, and your capacity to accomplish what you set out to do. It's the way you perceive yourself and the way you approach life.

It implies that you feel in charge of your life and accept and trust yourself. You have a positive opinion of yourself and know your skills and weaknesses. You can manage criticism, speak assertively, and set reasonable expectations and goals.

Self-confidence can manifest in various ways, such as how we communicate, our choices, and the risks we take. People with high self-confidence tend to be more assertive, optimistic, and resilient. They are more likely to take risks and pursue their goals, even in the face of challenges and setbacks. They also tend to have better mental and physical well-being and better relationships.

WHAT IS SELF-ESTEEM?

Self-confidence and self-esteem are related but distinct concepts.

Your belief in yourself and in your skills is referred to as self-confidence. This may vary based on the circumstances. It's common to feel more or less confident, depending on the situation.

Self-esteem is the state of appreciating and valuing oneself. Your life experiences and relationships with other people impact how you feel about yourself.

Self-esteem is a psychological concept that refers to your general opinion of your value or worth. It is your perception of yourself, both positive and negative, and it encompasses how you view and evaluate yourself. A **positive self-concept** and a **positive self-view** are characteristics of people with high self-esteem, whereas a negative self-concept and a negative self-view are characteristics of people with low self-esteem.

Self-concept, or your overall understanding of who you are, and self-esteem go hand in hand. It includes elements like self-worth, self-knowledge, self-image, and self-esteem.

Self-concept includes self-esteem, which expresses how you view and assess yourself.

Numerous elements can impact self-esteem, including early experiences, social interactions, and cultural norms. Additionally, it may be affected by a person's attitude, skills, and accomplishments. While those with low self-esteem are more self-critical, apprehensive, and prone to negative thinking, those with high self-esteem are more resilient, upbeat, and self-assured.

DEFENDING BOUNDARIES WITH SELF-ESTEEM

Self-confidence and self-esteem are essential life skills that help you in many ways, including establishing healthy boundaries and saying NO when necessary.

1. When you have self-confidence and self-esteem, you are more likely to trust your judgment and stand by your decisions. This can help reduce the guilt and anxiety you may feel when you say NO to someone.

2. You can trust that your decisions are based on your values and beliefs, and you can be confident in your ability to stand by them. Self-esteem also means you better understand your importance, which can be beneficial when making decisions and setting boundaries. This can make it easier to say NO and not feel guilty or anxious about it.

3. In addition to having confidence in your own decisions, having self-confidence and self-esteem can also make it easier for you to stick to your decisions. Self-confidence and self-esteem can give you the strength and courage to stand firm in your convictions and not be swayed by external pressures or expectations. This can help you stay true to your values and make it easier to say NO when needed.

4. Self-esteem can also help you set healthy boundaries and respect the boundaries of others. When you have a healthy sense of self-esteem, you are more likely to treat yourself and others with respect. This can help you be firmer and more direct when saying NO and sticking to your decisions.

5. When someone is trying to take advantage of you or when something isn't in your best interest, you'll be able to identify it. You'll be free from guilt or anxiety to step back and assess the circumstance.

Ultimately, self-confidence and self-esteem are crucial in helping you say NO.

These skills can give you the confidence to trust your judgment, stick to your decisions, and set healthy boundaries. This can help you make decisions and stand by them without feeling anxious or guilty.

In contrast, people with low self-esteem may find it harder to say NO because they may not see themselves as worthy of respect and may not believe they have the right to set boundaries. They may also fear rejection or disappointment and may be more likely to give in to the requests of others to avoid those things.

STRATEGIES FOR BUILDING CONFIDENCE & SELF-ESTEEM

Is it really possible?

Is it really possible to build self-confidence and self-esteem in the first place?

A significant body of research suggests that self-confidence and self-esteem can be developed over time.

Let me give you a few examples of such studies:

- According to a study that appeared in the Journal of ***Personality and Social Psychology***, persons who participated in things they excelled at, such as hobbies or sports, reported higher levels of self-esteem. The study also discovered that individuals who got good feedback from others also had higher self-esteem.

- Another study published in the Journal of ***Applied Psychology*** found that people who set and achieved goals experienced increased self-confidence. The study also discovered that individuals who received coaching and comments on improving their performance reported feeling more confident.

- A meta-analysis published in the Journal of ***Counseling Psychology*** showed that psychological interventions such as cognitive-behavioral therapy (CBT) and positive psychology interventions are effective in increasing self-esteem.

As you can see, research indicates that engaging in successful activities, setting and achieving goals, receiving encouraging feedback and coaching, and engaging in psychological interventions like cognitive-behavioral therapy and positive psychology interventions can all help people build their self-confidence and self-esteem over time.

Now, let me go into greater depth about these strategies.

What are those strategies?

It takes much more than just "dressing for success" or "faking it till you make it" to build self-confidence. You must dive deeper and make conscious, forward-thinking efforts. By practicing the below strategies consistently, you'll be able to develop unshakeable self-confidence and keep it for the long run.

Strategy #1) Overcome your critical inner voice

"Overcoming your critical inner voice" refers to overcoming negative self-talk and beliefs that can undermine self-confidence. These negative thoughts and beliefs can include things like *"I'm not good enough," "I'll never be successful,"* or *"I can't do this."* These thoughts can be deeply ingrained and difficult to change, but you can build self-confidence by learning to recognize and challenge them.

Dr. Lisa Firestone, the author of **Conquer Your Critical Inner Voice**, has suggested the bellow 4-step process to conquer your inner critic:

Step #1) Recognition: The first step is to become aware of your critical inner voice and the negative thoughts and beliefs it generates. This can involve paying attention to your thoughts throughout the day and noting when they are negative or self-defeating.

Determine what your critical inner voice is saying to you. Recognize that this thought process is distinct from your actual point of view.

Some common examples can be: *"I'm not smart enough," " I'm not worthy of love and happiness,"* or *"I'm too old/young to do this."*

Step #2) Understand the source of your voices: When people express their critical inner voices in this way, they frequently feel intensely and gain an understanding of the origin of their voice attacks. They are remarkably clear as they realize that the tone and content of their voice attacks are dated and familiar; they are expressing sentiments directed at them as kids. They frequently cite examples such as *"That's what my neighbor used to say," "That's the impression I got from my father,"* or *"That was the vibe in my family."* People can acquire self-compassion by understanding where their voices came from.

Step #3) Reframe: Next, reframe your critical inner voice more positively or realistically. This can involve looking for evidence that contradicts the negative thought or finding a more balanced perspective.

Reply back to your voice attacks.

For example, if earlier you were thinking something like, *"You're so stupid. Nobody is interested in hearing your thoughts. Just remain silent and remain in the background!"*; you may reframe it like, *"I'm not stupid! I have something worthwhile and important to say. Many people are curious about me and are concerned with what I think."*

After reframing this way, it is essential to make rational statements about who you are, who other people are, and what is true about your social environment. Then you may say, *"The world isn't a place where everyone else is brilliant, and I'm the sole stupid. No one evaluates us anymore; I'm no longer in primary school. In fact, I'm not a fool, and neither are most others. We are similar in that we are fascinating individuals with fascinating things to say about their thoughts and experiences."*

Step #4) Harnessing the power of your inner voice: As you journey towards self-discovery and growth, it is essential to understand their impact on your behavior after expressing and responding to your voices.

By expressing and responding to these voices, you gain valuable insight into how they shape your past and present experiences.

Understanding how your critical inner voice shapes your actions is a powerful tool in your quest to overcome self-limiting behaviors and unlock your full potential. Imagine, for instance, the individual who constantly hears the voice saying, *"I am stupid."* Through reflection, they may recognize instances when they held themselves back or lacked confidence due to this internal dialogue.

Embrace the power of your inner voice and use it to propel you toward greatness.

Step #5) Transcend Your Self-Imposed Boundaries: As you have identified the areas in which you limit yourself, it's time to take action and break free from the shackles of your own mind.

This is a pivotal moment in your journey toward self-discovery and growth.

The first step towards change is to stop indulging in the self-destructive behaviors that your critical inner voice encourages. For example, if you are shy and tend to avoid social interactions, it's time to step out of your comfort zone and consciously engage with others.

But it's not just about stopping negative behaviors; it's also about actively increasing positive behaviors that go against the recommendations of your critical inner voice. For example, striking up conversations with people, even if your inner critic tells you that you are not good enough.

By taking these small steps towards positive change, you are actively rewriting the script of your life and breaking free from the self-imposed boundaries that have held you back. Remember, every step you take towards change is a step closer to living the life you truly desire.

Embracing change can be daunting, especially when tackling those negative, self-doubting inner voices that hold us back. It's important to understand that as you begin to challenge and counteract these critical inner voices, they may initially become louder and more intense.

This is a normal part of the process. And it's crucial to push through this discomfort.

For some, these critical inner voices have become a familiar companion, and the thought of living without them can be unsettling. It's essential to remember that these voices do not define you and are not a necessary aspect of who you are.

Many people mistakenly believe that these inner voices are what keep them in check, but the reality is that they only hold you back and limit your potential. The more you act against them, the weaker their influence becomes.

Strategy #2) Unlock your potential by reflecting on your accomplishments

When we reflect on our accomplishments, we are reminded of the times when we felt proud and recognized, which can help to build self-confidence and counteract the negative inner critic.

Take some time to think about your life and list your top ten achievements. They can be big or small, but they are all significant to you.

For example:

- Graduating from college or university
- Landing a dream job or getting a promotion
- Running a marathon or completing a triathlon
- Starting a business or launching a successful product
- Overcoming a fear or phobia
- Completing a challenging hike or climb
- Learning a new skill or hobby

- Saving a significant amount of money
- Being recognized for volunteer work or community service
- Writing a book or publishing an article

Put this list somewhere where you can see it often, and spend a few minutes each day reflecting on the success you've already had. Allow these memories to make you feel good and remind you of who you truly are.

As a best-selling author and motivational speaker **Denis Waitley** said, *"To establish true self-confidence, we must concentrate on our successes and forget about the failures and the negatives in our lives."*

Doing this will remind you of your past successes and empower you to achieve more extraordinary things in the future.

Strategy #3) Stand tall, stand confident

We've all heard the phrase **"sit up straight,"** but did you know that good posture can actually boost your confidence?

When you sit up straight, you signal to your brain that you are in a powerful and assertive position, which can lead to a more positive and confident mindset. **Studies have shown a strong connection between body posture and emotions and that individuals can improve their mood and attitude by physically assuming confident postures**.

Research conducted at **Ohio State University** found that people who sat up straight were likelier to believe in their qualifications for a job than those who slouched at their desks.

A recent study examined how posture affects students' feelings about their performance. The study found that students who were anxious about math felt less capable of calculation when slouching, but sitting up straight gave them more confidence.

By maintaining good posture, you not only appear more confident, but you actually become more confident. This is because when you sit up straight, you align your spine correctly, which can help improve breathing, reduce muscle tension, and increase blood flow to the brain. These physiological changes can help you feel more alert and energized, which can contribute to feelings of confidence.

So, the next time you feel yourself slouching, remember to sit up straight and stand tall. Your mind and body will thank you for it.

Strategy #4) Don't strive to imitate someone else, be the unique and original version of yourself

Do you ever find yourself comparing yourself to others and feeling inadequate?

This is a common trait among people with low self-confidence. But it's important to remember that you are just as worthy and deserving as anyone else. The key is to develop an equality mentality.

It can be challenging to feel equal when we're constantly bombarded with images of perfection on social media, but it's important to remember that these images aren't based on reality. They're a curated and filtered version of someone's life.

Make a mental shift to an equality mentality, and you will quickly see an improvement in your self-confidence. Recognize that you are unique, and that's what makes you special. Stop comparing yourself to others, and start valuing yourself for who you are.

As **Marilyn Monroe** said, *"Wanting to be someone else is a waste of the person you are."*

Embrace your individuality and let it shine; that's the key to unlocking your true potential and confidence.

Strategy #5) Embrace the Uncomfortable

Step outside your comfort zone.

According to **Charlie Houpert**, the author of Charisma on Command, *"Confidence is ultimately about being comfortable in a wide variety of situations that would make most people feel uncomfortable."*

By taking small, daily steps to try new things, you will expand your comfort zone and feel more confident in various situations. This can be something as simple as striking up a conversation with someone at a cocktail party or trying a new sport. A few more examples can be:

- Public speaking
- Asking for a raise or promotion
- Confronting someone about a problem
- Negotiating a difficult deal or contract
- Leading a team or group
- Applying for a job or college
- Starting a business or new venture
- Traveling alone to a new place
- Overcoming a fear or phobia
- Take on a new hobby or challenge outside your comfort zone

Imagine standing confidently in front of an audience, delivering a speech with poise and grace. This is the power of embracing the uncomfortable. Public speaking may be uncomfortable for you, but by taking on this challenge and practicing, you can learn to control your nerves and become a confident speaker.

Asking for a raise or promotion can be intimidating, but it takes courage to put ourselves out there and ask for what we deserve. By having the guts to do it, we show ourselves and others that we are confident in our skills and worth as employees. It's a small step that can lead to significant gains.

Barrie Davenport, the author of Confidence Hacks, says, *"Low self-confidence isn't a life sentence. Self-confidence can be learned, practiced, and mastered–just like any other skill."*

So, don't let fear or discomfort keep you from reaching your full potential. Embrace the uncomfortable and watch as your self-confidence soars.

I hope now you got a clear idea of how self-confidence and self-esteem play a crucial role in helping you say NO. When you have a strong sense of self-worth, you are more likely to stand up for yourself and set boundaries.

Saying NO is not only essential for protecting your time and energy, but it also helps you build healthy relationships and achieve your goals. Remember, saying NO to what does not align with our values and priorities is a powerful way to take control of our lives.

So, have the confidence and self-esteem to say NO when necessary and trust in the power of your own voice.

EXERCISES FOR YOU

- **In the health area: *Set small, achievable fitness goals for yourself, then track your progress*.** This could be something as simple as committing to a daily walk or as challenging as training for a marathon. When we set and achieve our goals, it can boost our self-confidence and self-esteem. You can also set a nutrition goal, like eating more fruits and vegetables or drinking more water. Tracking your progress through a journal or an app, and celebrating small wins along the way, will help you stay motivated and remind yourself of your capabilities. This exercise can help build self-confidence and self-esteem by showing yourself that you can take control of your health and make positive changes in your life.

- **In the relationship area: *Practice active listening*.** This means genuinely paying attention to your partner when they speak and responding thoughtfully. This shows that you value and respect your partner's thoughts and feelings and allows you to better understand and connect with them. Additionally, practice expressing your own needs and wants clearly and assertively; this will help you feel more self-assured and confident in the relationship. This exercise can help build self-confidence and self-esteem by showing that you can communicate effectively in a relationship.

- **In the career area: *Take on a new project or responsibility at work.*** This could be something outside your comfort zone or that you have never done. You can remind yourself of your capabilities and potential by taking on new challenges and learning new skills. Set specific, measurable, achievable goals for the project or responsibility and track your progress. This can help build self-confidence and self-esteem by showing yourself that you can grow and succeed in your career. Once you have completed the project or responsibility, be sure to reflect on your accomplishments and share your successes with your colleagues and manager. This will increase your confidence and sense of achievement while demonstrating your capacity and aspirations to others.

- **In the money area: *Set and work towards financial goals.*** This could be something as simple as creating a budget or as challenging as paying off debt. Try to identify and challenge any limiting beliefs you may have about money, such as *"I will never be able to save enough"* or *"I am not good with money."* By demonstrating to yourself that you are capable of taking charge of your finances and making positive changes in your financial life, this exercise can help you develop self-confidence and self-esteem.

- **In the spiritual area: *Practice daily gratitude.*** This means taking a few minutes each day to reflect on the things in your life that you are thankful for. This can be done through journaling, meditating, or simply thinking about the things that bring you joy and happiness. Practicing gratitude can help shift your focus from negative thoughts to positive ones and can help to boost your self-confidence and self-esteem over time. Additionally, you can try to practice mindfulness, which is being present and aware of the current moment without judgment. This can help to improve self-awareness and self-acceptance and reduce stress. By demonstrating to yourself that you can be content and appreciate what you have in life, this activity can aid in developing self-confidence and self-esteem.

Good Luck!

6

Finding The 18th Camel Before Saying NO

In every conflict lies the seed of a solution.

- Idries Shah

18TH CAMEL - WHAT IS IT?

This Middle Eastern tale is about a guy who left 17 camels to his three kids. He left half of the camels to the oldest son, a third to the second son, and a ninth of the camels to his youngest son.

The three sons started negotiating since 17 cannot be divided in half. There is no division by three, also no division by nine. Tensions between brothers began to rise. Finally, out of despair, they went to a wise older woman for advice.

After giving their issue much attention, the wise old woman returned and stated, "Well, I don't know whether I can help you, but at least, if you want, you can have my camel. This way, you'll have 18 camels with you, and it might solve your problem."

Since half of 18 equals nine, the first son took his share, i.e., 9 camels.

A third of 18 is six; therefore, the second son took his third, i.e., 6 camels.

A ninth of 18 is two, and the youngest son took his 2 camels.

This way, they all got 9 + 6+ 2 = 17 camels.

Only one camel was remaining, and they returned it to the wise older woman!

BE WILLING TO SOLVE THE CONFLICT

If you give the above story some thought, I believe it has much in common with the challenging conversations we engage in.

They begin like 17 camels with no hope of resolution. Like the sensible older woman, we must somehow **take a step back from those circumstances to objectively assess them and identify the 18th camel**.

Every time we experience conflict in our lives, finding the 18th camel becomes exceptionally crucial.

Whatever the cause of arguments and confrontations at home or at business, saying NO right away is never a good idea. During a steamy discussion, we become more reactive and angrily reject all the proposals proposed by the other person. We firmly show our disagreement with the person in front, which is never a good thing to do. You may resolve disputes constructively while maintaining and expanding your relationships.

Any healthy relationship will have conflict. After all, it is unrealistic to expect two people to agree on everything all of the time. Because when you try to avoid conflict, you keep rejecting the person in your mind. You always seem to disagree with the person. The goal is to learn how to resolve disputes healthily rather than fearing or avoiding them.

No matter how hard you try, conflict is an unavoidable aspect of life. You are mistaken if you believe you can have a relationship without friction or dispute. Conflict in relationships is inevitable, given the diversity of every human person.

Similar to the above story, in real-life situations, making difficult decisions often requires individuals to think outside the box and to be willing to consider unconventional solutions. It also needs individuals to be able to make trade-offs and to be ready to accept that there may not be a perfect solution.

You might often need to say NO, ready to accept what is correct at that moment. This will enable you to take ownership of the outcome. And emphasize the importance of standing up for what you believe in, even when it is difficult.

This determination and the ability to stand up for what is right, even when difficult, is key to making difficult decisions in real life.

It's all about our responsibility for how and when we say YES or NO.

William Ury discusses a method called **"the third side"** in one of his TED talks, which aids in resolving conflicts in various situations. He states - *"When we think about and describe the conflict, we always see two sides: Arabs versus Israelis, labor versus management, husband versus wife, Republicans versus Democrats. But we don't frequently notice that there is always a third side, and that third side is* ***'us,'*** *the surrounding community, friends, allies, family members, and neighbors. And we have the potential to be extremely beneficial."*

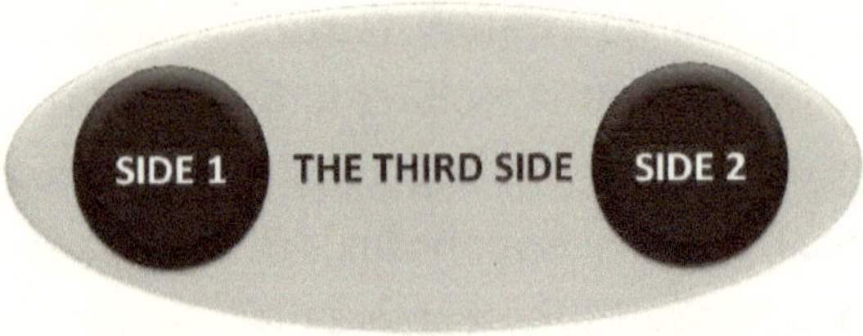

The most essential method in which **"the third side"** might assist is to remind the parties of what is truly at stake.

For the sake of the children, the family, the community, and the future, let us put aside our differences and start talking. Because it's pretty simple to lose perspective when we're embroiled in a disagreement.

It's pretty simple to react. We, humans, are reaction machines. But remember the saying - ***"when angry, you will make the best speech you will ever regret."***

The third side facilitates a deep dive into our inner self, i.e., a point of view from which we can keep our eyes on the prize. We must recognize that we are here to see if we can find a method to end the suffering caused by our disagreements.

That's the role of **the third side**, to help the parties go and churn the inner self.

When standing on **the third side,** you should be extra vigilant in taking appropriate action. You often need to say YES for the benefit of others and yourself, and other times you have to say NO for the same reasons.

PROTECTIVE SHIELD OF NO VS. THE SWORDS OF YES

Actually, the real issue of not being able to correctly measure when to say YES or when to say NO starts just from a young age.

While you're young, you always have the wildest ideas. You wanted to explore places, meet with your friends (but outside your house), try to have a fun time with your friends, etc.

But there was **a word** that almost all the time broke all your feelings of fun and excitement. You never wanted to hear that word from anyone. Even though it only has two letters, it's incredibly potent.

Yes! You got it! I am talking about the word NO.

Can you also co-relate to yourself with the following:

- Can I have more sweets? NO!
- May I go out and spend time with my friends on Saturday night? NO!
- Can I dress up like Spiderman and go to school? NO!!

Did it remind you of something from your past? A similar story?

As you age, the word NO comes to mean rejection and refusal. You were so furious with your parents that you immediately rushed upstairs, grabbed two items and two handbags, and packed everything up before saying, *"you know, I'm leaving. Yes, I'll leave right now. I'm getting out of here and never want to come back. You never let me enjoy myself. You have no idea what fun is!"*

But here's the thing - when you are young, you're ignorant and lacking in knowledge. And your parents justify their refusal with solid reasons:

- You can not eat more sweets - because it's not good for your tooth and stomach!
- You can not go out and spend time with your friends on Saturday night - because you should not waste time and keep studying!

- You can not dress up like Spiderman and go to school - because good boys go to school in proper school uniform!

As we grow up and mature, we become aware of things and realize why our parents' NO was beneficial for us. We understand that many times NO is a better choice.

That's why all we need to learn is - how to use the power of the word NO to grow. **Understanding when and why to say NO is just as vital as knowing how to say NO, as it opens up long and short-term opportunities**.

Many of us may have experienced several situations in which NO was intended to protect us, either initially or in hindsight. We later understand that the word NO is primarily a defense mechanism against the dangers of the word YES.

Using Both - The Defensive Shield of NO and The Sword of YES

When you read this chapter, I want you to consider the word NO quite differently now than you did in the past.

The **CEO and co-founder** of **ThreeSixtyEight**, ***Kenny Nguyen,*** introduced the idea of the ***swords of YES*** and the ***shield of NO*** in his **"The Art of Saying No"** TedTalk and discussed how to use the power of NO to progress in life.

Based on that, **I want you to see the word NO as a complement to the swords of YES, a defensive shield that will keep you safe.**

Many people use the ***swords of YES***, but there are very few people who use the ***shield of NO***. Because nobody wants to use the *NO-shield.* They believe they are discarding someone or something by acting in this way. Considering that the word NO means to reject someone literally. Nobody wants to be abandoned by a loved one, a friend, or even themself.

Despite this, there seem to be a lot of *YES-man* in the world. Public icons like **Martin Luther King** and **Nelson Mandela** responded positively to every opportunity presented to them.

YES-people show that they are willing to assist you, and they present you as a trustworthy resource. If you are a *YES-man,* this habit frequently allows you to explore new ideas and endeavors.

I'll go into more detail on this lovely subject shortly, but here let me explain why it's essential to leverage the power of both YES and NO. ***If YES is the sword you can use to combat any situation, NO is the shield you may use to protect yourself from any damage that might befall you***.

Knowing when and why to say NO is just as important as knowing how to say it. This opens up the gate for better opportunities and offers in the long term.

Before explaining this further, let me take a moment and present **Kenny Nguyen's story** he shared during his TedTalk.

It goes like this:

"At big fish presentations, we face a very similar situation where months ago, we got an amazing offer to be on a show called ***Shark Tank****. It's a reality TV show where you go on the show and pitch to a panel of celebrity investors. And the marketing itself is worth hundreds of thousands of dollars, but in return for pitching to investors, they potentially can give you X amount of dollars for X amount of your company."*

Now let's see the moment when Kenny did not act on his inner voice. He continued:

"It was literally one of the coolest things you can imagine. Being even asked on the show consider where a young startup. And I remember being so stoked, but something in my heart said - ***DON'T DO IT****. But you know, I'm not gonna listen to it, so we went through the first round of interviews. The second batch of interviews came*

*around, and the noise started coming from my heart even louder, and said - "***NO Kenny, DON'T DO IT.***" But once again, I was thinking about the money, so I didn't listen to the voice, and altogether the voice stopped. And so, with the third and final round of revisions coming around, that's when the voice didn't appear."*

"I remember taking my team out that day to lunch, knowing that later that day, we'll have a phone conversation with the executive producers on accepting our bid to go to Los Angeles to film the show. And we were having so much fun, and we're just chatting saying - 'what we're going to do in LA, what we're going to do with all the money we're going to get, what we're gonna do with publicity, how does it feel like to be a celebrity entrepreneur.' It was literally so exhilarating."

And now, let's see how Kenny's gut feeling turned everything around. He further said:

*"But then I got a call while at lunch. It changed my life. I stepped outside, took the call, and it was one of my mentors. She said - '***Kenny, what does your heart tell you to do?***' Because she can tell my voice, I wasn't confident in my decision. Something started ringing in me. I didn't say anything back, and she asked again - 'Kenny, what does your heart tell you to do?' And that's when I realized something. My heart was screaming out for me, and I didn't listen to it. I sacrificed my ethics as an entrepreneur of rather build the company rather than chasing the money. And that's not what I built our*

*company on, and you can imagine how I felt to walk back in. I know several members of my team members are here today; remember how grim my face was as I walked in and said - '**guys, we're not going to go on the show.**'"*

And finally, the lesson from his talk:

*"While you might think that's a loss, there is a method to the madness, and there is a lesson that taught me that money can never buy. That lesson is - '**following your gut feeling.**' So many times, do we take the swords of YES, slashing right through the opportunities of life, crushing right through. But we sometimes realize some obstacles we just can't cut."*

"When do you use your shield to protect you?"

"And that's the trick - when to use your sword versus your shield. And you can learn and develop that by developing your gut feeling. And you learn to develop your gut feeling - by turning down big opportunities in the short term for even bigger opportunities in the long term."

From Nguyen's story, we realize the importance of listening to our instincts in YES-NO situations. In these circumstances, we must employ both the ***swords of YES*** and the protective ***shield of NO***.

It all comes down to establishing your gut instinct as to whether you should use your swords of YES to overcome difficulties or your protective shield of NO to protect yourself. You might miss the significant opportunities in the short term by following your gut instinct, but you'll be setting yourself up for far greater opportunities in the long run.

You may be closing one door when you refuse something. However, you are also creating space for personal development and advancement for the other individual and yourself by opening a new entry for more excellent prospects.

THE PROS AND CONS OF BEING A PEOPLE-PLEASER

Being a people pleaser can positively and negatively affect an individual. On the one hand, it can lead to solid relationships, a sense of belonging, and personal growth and learning opportunities.

On the other hand, it can also result in feelings of resentment, neglecting one's own needs, and potentially becoming a doormat for others to walk all over.

People pleasers are highly valued by managers and colleagues due to their willingness to always help out and their dependability. They are often considered the "go-to" person in the office because they never say NO, earning them the nickname of **"YES-MAN."**

While being a people pleaser can have advantages, such as being well-liked by colleagues and being seen as generous and humble, it can also negatively impact one's work-life balance as one struggles to manage personal and professional commitments.

Let me explain a few important pros and cons of being a YES-MAN.

Pros of being a YES-MAN

1. **Builds and maintains strong relationships:** One of the main pros of being a people pleaser is building and maintaining strong relationships. By constantly putting others' needs and wants before one's own, individuals can create a sense of trust and loyalty within their relationships. This can lead to a robust support system, which can be beneficial in both personal and professional contexts.

2. **Gives you the opportunity for growth:** Another pro is the opportunity for personal growth and learning. Individuals are often exposed to new perspectives and experiences they may not have otherwise encountered by constantly trying to please others. This can broaden one's horizons and a greater understanding of the world around them.

3. **Depicts you as a trustworthy source:** Being a YES-MAN is often associated with being dependable and reliable. When individuals are always willing to say YES to requests, their colleagues and management see them as valuable resources. They are often the first to be approached for new projects and are expected to volunteer for tasks others may not be interested in. This can lead to being valued by the company and being rewarded for their hard work and dedication.

4. Positively impacts your reputation: Saying YES to new opportunities and tasks can increase a positive reputation in the workplace in several ways:

- By consistently saying YES and being willing to help, colleagues and managers will view you as a team player ready to go above and beyond for the team's good. This can lead to increased trust and respect, which can help to establish a positive reputation.

- By taking on additional responsibilities, you demonstrate a strong work ethic and a willingness to learn new skills. This can lead to increased recognition and appreciation by management and colleagues.

- You are more likely to be included in important projects and meetings by saying YES to new opportunities. This can lead to increased visibility and influence within the company.

- Being a YES-MAN, you demonstrate a positive attitude and a willingness to take on new challenges. This can lead to increased respect and admiration by colleagues and management, which can help establish a positive reputation.

Cons of being a YES-MAN

1. Burnout: Saying YES to every opportunity and request can lead to taking on too much work, which can cause physical and emotional exhaustion. When individuals take on more than they can handle, they may feel overwhelmed and stressed. This can lead to decreased productivity, a lack of motivation, and physical symptoms such as fatigue and headaches.

2. **Neglecting personal needs:** Saying YES to others can lead to ignoring one's own needs, resulting in resentment and unhappiness. Individuals may feel undervalued and unimportant when they put others' needs before their own. This can lead to feelings of anger and frustration, as well as difficulties in personal and professional relationships.

3. **Being taken advantage of:** People pleasers may be more likely to be taken advantage of by others who know they will always be willing to put others' needs before their own. When individuals are always ready to help, they may be more likely to be taken advantage of by colleagues who know they will always be there to lend a hand. This can lead to a cycle of being used and taken for granted, which can be detrimental to personal and professional relationships.

4. **Lack of assertiveness:** Constantly saying YES can make it difficult for individuals to assert themselves and set boundaries. Individuals who are always willing to please others may find it hard to say NO when asked to do something uncomfortable or feel overwhelmed. This can lead to difficulties in personal and professional relationships because individuals may feel resentful and taken advantage of. Furthermore, they may find it hard

to advocate for themselves and their own needs, which can lead to being overlooked and undervalued.

5. **Loss of autonomy:** Constantly saying yes can lead to a loss of independence, as individuals may feel pressured to do things they don't want to do and may not have the freedom to make their own choices. When individuals are always saying YES, they may feel like they are not in control of their own lives, which can lead to feelings of powerlessness and dissatisfaction.

6. **Damaged relationships:** Saying YES to everything can damage relationships as people-pleasers may find themselves in situations where they are unable to properly care for themselves and their own well-being, which can lead to feelings of anger and frustration. When individuals put others' needs before their own, they may neglect their own well-being, which can lead to problems in personal and professional relationships.

In conclusion, while being a people pleaser can have its benefits, such as strong relationships and opportunities for personal growth, it also has its downsides, such as feelings of resentment and the potential for being taken advantage of. A better understanding of when to say YES and when to say NO is crucial for maintaining a healthy work-life balance and for protecting one's own well-being.

It is essential to carefully evaluate each situation and consider the consequences before deciding. It's also important to communicate our decision clearly and respectfully. It's not always easy to say NO, but learning to do it politely and professionally can prevent misunderstandings and hard feelings.

Additionally, setting healthy boundaries and learning how to communicate them effectively can help people-pleasers to establish a balance between being helpful and avoiding burnout.

This way, one can better understand when to say YES and NO and make decisions that align with their values and priorities.

In today's fast-paced world, getting caught up in a never-ending cycle of commitments, responsibilities, and expectations is easy. However, saying YES to everything can lead to burnout, stress, and feeling overwhelmed. Learning to effectively say NO is an essential skill that can help you manage your time and energy, prioritize your goals, and maintain a healthy work-life balance.

But how to do that? What are the techniques and strategies for effectively saying NO?

The next chapter explores all these proven techniques for saying NO in a confident, assertive, and respectful way. Whether you're dealing with unreasonable demands from coworkers, trying to avoid overextending yourself, or simply looking to set healthy boundaries, these techniques will help you communicate your needs and boundaries effectively.

So, buckle up and continue reading...

7

Proven Techniques for Effectively Saying NO

When we say no to the things that don't matter, we say yes to the things that do.

- Dave Ramsey

THE REAL PROBLEM

In his book, **The Power of a Positive No, William Ury** has defined the problem of saying NO into 3 parts: **Accommodate, Attack & Avoid.**

Accommodate: *This involves saying YES to the request and adjusting to accommodate the other person. This may include making sacrifices or going out of your way to accommodate the request.*

Attack: *This involves saying NO in an aggressive or confrontational manner, either by denying the request outright or arguing against it. This approach can lead to conflict and negative consequences.*

Avoid: *This involves avoiding the request altogether, either by ignoring it, avoiding the person who made the* *request, or avoiding the situation altogether. This approach can be passive or evasive and can lead to feelings of guilt or frustration.*

According to him, these are not only three distinct strategies. One usually overflows into the other. We ultimately fall victim to the **"three-A trap."** He further says, **"we are like a mouse caught in a maze, rushing from one box to another but never getting to the cheese."**

So, let's understand in detail how we blindly fall into this trap, and it becomes tough for us to come out of it without applying the right strategies.

THE REAL SOLUTION

Every day, we receive a deluge of requests, emails, invitations, and direct appeals. All of these things have an impact on how our day goes. The choices we make will immediately affect the obligations we will keep and the goals we will achieve.

It is a known fact that trying to handle too many tasks at once can prevent you from being effective. Because of this, learning the art of saying NO can drastically increase productivity.

Saying NO, though, can be extremely painful.

However, you may take control over your work schedules and what you want to do with them if you learn to say NO gently. And it is precisely the lesson we must learn in life.

You must be thinking - *what's the big deal about saying NO?*

It's never a fun task to say NO to someone because it can hurt, upset, or disappoint them.

Second, expressing NO wrong could harm your relationship with that person, making it harder for you to work with them again.

Therefore, this chapter will teach you how to quit pleasing others and master the skill of saying NO compassionately to help you maintain your professional relationships.

Let's consider the following steps for stating NO:

1) Determine Your YES

Understanding what you are saying YES to and its effects on you is necessary before you can get better at saying NO.

However, every opportunity you decline with a NO is a YES to something else you'd prefer to undertake or something that will be more important to you in the long run. If you don't know what you want specifically, you won't be able to say NO when under pressure.

Therefore, your first responsibility should be to consider your response when you are under pressure to say YES and believe that giving in is more manageable than standing your ground.

Imagine, for instance, that you have received an invitation to participate in your company's CSR initiative. You might have to spend your weekends working on campaigns if you say YES to this chance. Additionally, you won't have much time to spend with your family.

By focusing on this truth, you will gain the ability to say NO and maintain your priorities.

2) Refrain From Saying Direct YES

If you have doubts about the opportunity you have been presented with and are driven to say YES, **DON'T DO THAT!**

Abstain from going to a direct YES!

It would be best if you asked for a day to consider the opportunity before responding. After a thorough self-reflection on your obligations, you'll be able to determine if the presented commitment is a feasible addition to your calendar.

You will undoubtedly have the chance to consider the best way to say NO if you give your decision some thought the night before.

3) Learn the Difference Between *Whether* and *How*

Thoughts like *"I would like to say NO, but there's no way I can picture saying NO to my dad, supervisor, colleague, or my loved ones"* may occasionally cross our minds.

Even before we start a conversation with the other, we weaken our purpose of saying NO.

When your best friend asks you for help, you may think, *"I don't see how I can say NO."* Even though you know you don't have the time right now, saying NO seems impossible as your mind is overtaken by guilt and anxiety.

Thus, you compromise and agree to say YES!

The guilt, frustration, and rage soon followed since, at that moment, saying YES was the last thing you wanted to do. This frequently occurs for many of us every day.

It also results from the widespread practice of mistaking **whether** something should be done and **how** to achieve it.

If you deeply churn the scenario, you will know that you are actually not focused on **WHETHER** you should say NO or not; you are more worried about **HOW** to say NO (or, maybe, you don't know how to say NO). Since you don't know how to say NO in those situations, you end up saying YES. You tell yourself, *"It's OK with me,"* to make yourself feel better.

Let me give you a solution to such situations -

First and foremost, you should consider what you want to accomplish in this case. When the WHETHER question is answered, you can think about the HOW, which might be simpler than your anxieties had you believed!

4) Place Two YESses & a NO in the Middle

Making a NO sandwiched between two YESses will increase the appeal of your NO. It's an excellent way to clarify what you've previously agreed to.

For instance, if your supervisor requests that you work on the weekend, but you cannot do so due to family commitments.

If so, you should let your manager know what these obligations are. This will be your **first YES.**

Then you can justify why being away from your family keeps you from working on the weekend. Your NO will be highlighted in that.

And finally, you can ask if there are any other ways you can help out on the business front by reiterating your dedication to the company and your work. This will be your **last YES**.

For example, you can say to your supervisor something like below:

- *I appreciate your trust in me and am always eager to support the company's needs. However, I have prior family commitments that cannot be rescheduled for the weekend. If needed, I am willing to make up for it by taking on additional responsibilities during the week.*

- *I understand the project's urgency and am eager to contribute whenever possible. Unfortunately, I have family commitments on the weekend that take precedence. Would it be possible to arrange my workload so I can complete the tasks during the week and still meet my family obligations?*

- *I am committed to my job and always willing to go the extra mile. However, my family commitments on the weekend are non-negotiable. Is there anything else I can assist with during the week to ensure that the project stays on track?*

Using this indirect NO technique, you may respect your time while maintaining good working relationships.

5) Avoid Using Limp Phrases

Remember not to make mistakes, as the word NO can be compelling!

We often yield our swords of YES and slash into it even when an opportunity is not meant for us. As a result, we typically become frustrated with ourselves.

You must understand that using a sword to slash your opponent is not always necessary; you may also need a shield to defend yourself. And the word NO can serve as a barrier to keep you from taking on those unnecessary obligations.

However, to achieve it, you must confidently yield that shield!

Avoid saying things like *"I don't think I can"* or *"I'm not sure."*

When weak sentences are used in place of a NO, they are commonly interpreted as a YES.

So, **when it's time to say NO, say NO!**

6) If Needed, Repeat Yourself

Saying NO again is best if the other person pushes back after you say it the first time.

If your previous response included an explanation, you can reiterate it or respond NO. You can gently refuse any request, and you'll frequently need to be firm to clarify your point.

Dear friend, by mastering the proven techniques mentioned above for effectively saying NO, you empower yourself to control your time, energy, and priorities. This skill is essential for leading a balanced and fulfilling life, as it allows you to set healthy boundaries and prioritize what matters most to you.

So, don't be afraid to put these techniques into practice and take back control of your life. The confidence and peace of mind that come with assertively expressing your needs and boundaries are priceless.

8

Say NO to Say YES

If I am not for myself, who will be for me? If I am only for myself, what am I? And if not now, when?

- Hillel

MY INSPIRING STORY

One day I got a call from one of my neighbors -

She - *"Hello Ravi, today, from 3:00 PM to 6:00 PM, my husband and I are going to a party, and as you know, my son is too naughty, and we cannot take him with us. So, if you don't mind, please do me a favor and take care of him when we are out? Is that OK for you?"*

Me *(talking to myself in frustration)* - *"I already about knew this. Today is Sunday, and again she will ask me to take care of her son. She will take advantage of my kindness."*

This was not the first time she was taking advantage; she used to call me every now and then to ask to take care of her son.

I talked to myself - *"Oh my gosh! I have a call at 3:45 and need to prepare a presentation for next week's webinar."*

I did this whole mental calculation, and do you know what my response was?

Me (to her) - ***Sure. No problem!***

After that, I put down the phone and began to speak aloud in my brain.

At 3:00 PM, I went to her house and spent three hours playing with her son, so I could not give my full attention to my work!

I was on a hyperdrive of aggravation - ***I'm doing this, but why?***

I'm too busy, and I did it!

So, my friend, do you relate to my story about when you agreed to something and started babbling in your head afterward?

Does my story seem like your own story?

- Have you ever taken a job that you should have gotten paid for but didn't?
- Have you ever told a small white lie and felt terrible about it?

- Do you say NO to a request, a volunteer role, or even something at your church or temple?
- Have you ever thought of saying NO but ended up saying YES? If so, how did that make you feel?

If you consider my story, whose fault was there? Did I do anything wrong, or was that lady unfair to me? What do you think?

It was also a time when things in my personal life began to change, and I thought I was saying YES a lot. This had a profound impact on my well-being, leading to feelings of frustration and unhappiness. My mood was negative; I was waking up frequently in the morning, struggling to fall asleep, and feeling discontent with my world, which directly resulted from my tendency to always say YES.

This is something I frequently refer to as **people-pleasing**. And I believe everyone is prone to people-pleasing, which is now a widespread issue. This is what we learn growing up.

Affirmation, Acceptance, and Approval are the **three A's**, and I characterize people-pleasing as: **We seek externally, to the outside world, for the three A's rather than looking within ourselves for Affirmation, Acceptance, and Approval**. And when we look for those three A's from other sources, we frequently say YES at the expense of ourselves.

We weaken our own power by saying YES to something at the expense of ourselves to get

affirmation, acceptance, or approval. Individually, as a culture, and most importantly economically, it compromises our integrity and drains our energy.

We frequently accept jobs that don't fit our main objective but do so because we believe it to be the right thing to do rather than negotiating over the salary offered.

So how did we learn this?

- It is passed down to us from our parents from birth. They entirely fueled that by heaping praise and encouraging us to believe that if we say YES to something, we will receive acceptance, approval, and affirmation.

- We learn it through our classmates and from the media as well. People will like you much more if you always say YES to them, irrespective of what you really feel about that.

Naturally, I observe it in my own life and the lives of my friends, relatives, neighbors, and coworkers. It hurts so badly. In terms of discovering who we are and how to become more powerful, we still have a long way to go. **Now is when we must practice saying NO when we really mean it**.

So here's the problem: It becomes challenging for us to say NO. Why?

Because we worry that if we refuse, people won't love or accept us. Our close friends, family, and the other individuals who matter to us won't accept us. Or we risk rejection if we decline someone or something.

Additionally, I believe that sometimes we are frightened of missing out on chances that might come our way in the future if we turn down something that doesn't serve our primary purpose or mission in life, whatever that may be.

And then we simply say YES because it seems the easiest and the best option at that moment. But in reality, that is NOT the best option!

Further, if you say NO after having said YES for a while, let me tell you from personal experience that you sometimes encounter many negative consequences. This is because people are accustomed to taking advantage of you, and if they hear NO from you, they get angry. They already assume that you will say YES.

Therefore, when you say NO, it might significantly affect your friendships and family connections. It can disrupt working relationships, produce a lot of conflicts, and cause internal suffering.

The easiest solution

The easiest solution to handle these moments is to just think of all the scenarios that will occur when you say NO. You can consider many what-ifs like:

- *What if I decline the salary offered and counteroffer something that is $30,000 higher and precisely what I want because I deserve it?*

- *What if I say - You know what, I really hate washing clothes and dishes, cooking food and cleaning, so we're going to divide up the responsibilities equally, and here's what I'm going to do, and here's when I'm not going to do anything.*

- *What if you tell your friend that you're sick of having to travel across town to see them and suggest they meet you somewhere nearby, at your house, or even halfway?*

So, my friend, I propose that refusing can be a type of independence and emancipation. **Saying NO may be a sort of freedom and liberty because it gives you more room to say YES to the things that are truly meaningful and profoundly essential to you.**

When you start saying NO, you have more space to say YES to your inner self.

For example:

- You suddenly have more time by declining jobs or volunteer work that you don't genuinely enjoy.

- Saying NO to people who drain you of your authenticity gives you the freedom to meet friends or hang out with family that genuinely accept you for who you are and love you without conditions.

When you say NO, it can also help you to be more honest with yourself.

EXERCISES FOR YOU

Exercise 1: *I encourage you to write down the things you might want to refuse to experience greater freedom and improve your self-awareness. Identify 10 such things.*

Exercise 2: Read aloud the below bullet points and try to understand and feel the intentions behind them:

- **I would always have more options than I think, and one of those options is always *"saying NO."***
- **I promise to be sincere and genuine.** Remember that speaking the truth is a way of expressing NO when you really mean YES to what you want.
- **I'll be out front when I need or want something.** (I learned during several webinars that individuals are incredibly vague, manipulative, and unclear whether they say YES or NO; everyone else finds that to be really distressing. It's essential to be clear about what you believe or desire.)
- **I'm going to live without grudges.** Keep in mind that by saying NO, you can live in freedom rather than feeling burdened by obligations.
- **I'll respect my need for relaxation**.
- **I won't apologize for refusing**.
- **To appease others, I will not compromise my ethics.** Because it undermines your fundamental self

when you say YES to please others and then kick yourself for not saying NO.

- **I won't agree to anything that will weaken my authority**.

- **If I feel confused, I will take some time.** (You can think about saying - *"I haven't decided what to do about your proposal. I need some time to think about this. In a day, I'll reply to you."* Then honestly, ask yourself: *"Does this match my mission or responsibilities?"* If the answer is NO, just pass this up and say, *"No thanks, I'm not available."*)

- **Only when I really mean it will I say YES.** Then I'll be able to fulfill that promise with clarity, intention, and purpose.

Now, let me take you to another aspect of saying NO, i.e., how to say NO when you have already said YES to something or someone.

In my next chapter, I'll reveal a few techniques and tips that will help you when you are confused about how to say NO because you've already said YES to someone for the sake of anything (maybe due to peer pressure, you swayed away with the emotions or you did not want to create any hot moments at that time) and now you feel guilty about it and realize that you should have said NO in the first place itself.

Continue reading...

9

Saying NO After Saying YES

It is easier to stay out than get out.

- Mark Twain

WHY ARE YOU UNABLE TO BACK OUT

Consider this scenario:

You wholeheartedly agreed to a significant project. You believe in this project, and the others are glad to have you on board.

You were in an excellent mood, excited, and ready to jump in.

After a while, your life takes an unexpected turn.

Everything is fine, but things have changed. There is less time and bandwidth available. You are stressed just thinking about this assignment and what it will take to complete it.

You have already said YES to it, and people rely on you. You also take pride in keeping commitments, no matter what.

But this current situation leads you to a tumultuous emotional storm of regret, failure, dread, and fear. You are worried about appearing weak, letting people down, and damaging your image.

How do you overcome this situation?

A similar thing happened to me sometime back when I got a call from one of my clients.

She called me and explained her situation -

"Since I am very good at maintaining my daily routines and consistent with my work, a local community group asked me a favor to create a course and training program on the subject ***'how to maintain our daily life routine'*** *for teenagers' mentorship program."*

"I accepted the request because I was working part-time and believed I had enough time and could do it perfectly."

"But since then, I've been offered a full-time job, and between that, house chores, grocery shopping, taking care of my family, etc. I'm completely exhausted now, and that dreaded training course is staring me down."

"I don't want to break my promise and damage my career and reputation, but I'm absolutely overloaded."

Have you ever encountered similar situations and hesitated to say NO after saying YES?

If yes, let's solve this issue and learn how to back out gracefully.

DEVELOPING A POWERFUL NO

We've all been there - getting a new job, an innovative idea, a relationship, or a request.

When an opportunity presents itself, we know deep down that we don't want to be a part of it, but we can't seem to say NO when declining costs are cheap. Or we ignore the little voice in our heads that tells us we're not sure we're making the correct decision.

The word NO is difficult to say. It's the most challenging word to speak for some individuals. Saying NO implies asserting yourself, leaving an opportunity, and maybe disappointing or even harming another person - all of which are pretty frightening to our communal, people-pleasing thinking.

Of course, saying NO after saying YES is far more difficult. However, we frequently overlook that the person who will have to say NO tomorrow is the same person who is saying YES now.

How much anxiety, animosity, and conflict could we avoid if we learned to like the word NO?

Obviously, the answer is **a lot**.

Saying NO is a skill that we should all strive for. NO is a powerful concept that can change your life. **The ability to say NO is a superpower**.

So, let's explore what to do if you've already said YES and are now in a situation you don't want to be a part of. Let's learn how to get out of obligations with the least fuss possible, strengthening your relationships and feeling of self.

Even **before you try to say NO, you must**:

- **Make sure you know you have a genuine desire to stay out**

Take some time to carefully analyze your reasons for quitting before considering dropping out of a commitment.

Sometimes we want to back out of a commitment because we can't fulfill our promise. There are instances when we feel like quitting because we are momentarily overburdened, annoyed, or dissatisfied with a particular job.

Instead of attempting to address the underlying reasons for the stress, sometimes it feels easier to abandon the commitment totally.

I've been in such situations many times in my life. When I feel more stressed and overwhelmed, I get a strong desire to break my commitment. The idea of quitting is a way for me to reclaim power.

But that doesn't mean that walking away is always the best option. It just indicates that my mind recognizes that something needs to change. Perhaps I need to settle a disagreement with somebody working on the project. Maybe I need to develop better procedures and routines to establish control and do my task efficiently.

In some circumstances, though, desiring to back out is a clue that you should step out.

If no level of planning or implementation can help you get the job done correctly, you're likely just too stretched out. If you enjoy everyone involved in the project but are unwilling to spend time with others, you can certainly not give them your best.

Alternatively, if your sentiments about the commitment have significantly changed — you no longer feel engrossed in the aim, or your impression of the people involved has deteriorated — then backing out is almost certainly the best option.

- **Evaluate your reasons for saying NO**

✓ Are you considering leaving just to avoid performing the task or having a challenging interaction? Or,
✓ Do you feel compelled to quit due to your inability to deliver? Or,
✓ Because your understanding of the scenario has changed?

I urge you to write down your reasons for deciding to leave, where they originate from, and what you may do mainly to resolve them. I also suggest discussing this with a few trustworthy friends or mentors to gain additional viewpoints.

Be utterly truthful as you go through this activity. Don't be shy. Make a thorough assessment of your causes for leaving, and investigate them to discover more about your desire to say NO.

By the conclusion, you'll have a greater understanding of your situation and thorough knowledge of why you want to stop. **And you'll almost definitely know just what to do**.

If it comes out that your desire to leave is a kind of escape, you might consider reconnecting to the endeavor with a fresh approach or attitude.

You may, for example:

✓ Collaborate with your partners to make the job more practical and productive.
✓ Could plan meetings to address any problems or issues of uncertainty.
✓ Could take on new obligations to keep yourself engaged.
✓ Could devise a few routines to help you stay focused on the task.

Whatever the option, make an effort to make the improvements that will entice you to continue.

In another sense, use your desire to leave **as a signal to address the issues that must be solved**. That is perhaps the most valuable aspect of wishing to say NO.

However, if you find that saying NO is your only alternative, you must consider a critical factor - **THE PRICE YOU HAVE TO PAY**.

- **Be aware of the price you have to pay**

Every NO you say may come with a cost you must eventually pay.

✓ It could be an individual you may disappoint, such as an employer, a friend, a long-term partner, or perhaps even yourself.
✓ It could be an opportunity to learn, grow, or make a new connection that you pass up.
✓ It could also harm your reputation, relationships, or future possibilities.

So the critical question must be answered: **How much do those things cost? And do they outweigh the benefits of being relieved of the commitment?**

It is not necessary to always say NO when you feel the need to pull out. Sometimes your instinct is correct, and you should listen to it. However, it is critical to understand the costs.

✓ What do you give up by keeping your commitment?
✓ What do you lose if you abandon it?
✓ How high are such costs to you?

If you do the math, you'll feel more confident that you've made the appropriate decision.

If you complete this exercise and conclude that saying NO is the only best course of action, GREAT!

Instead of making a choice based on a conditioned response, like so many people do, you're doing it now with your wide-open eyes.

Then comes the final point - **DELIVER YOUR MESSAGE.**

DELIVER YOUR NO

- **Be truthful while also being courteous**

It's never easy to retract your commitment after you've made it. You're going to let someone down, mess up the flow, or create new issues. That is how it has worked so far for millions of people.

However, you can lessen that conflict by saying NO thoughtfully and calculatedly.

So, how do we do that?

Let's learn it now.

- **Convey it in a way that causes the least amount of stress possible**

Let me give you an example that happened a few years back when I was working with *Susan*, one of my clients. I had committed my time to her as a life coach. But soon, I found that it was really not going to work with her, and I needed to say NO to her.

Before talking to her, I had done all my math and calculations. And I finally concluded to say NO to working with her.

I started by saying to her - *"Hi Susan, I wanted to talk to you about my engagement with you."*

And, then, I continued - *"It may be disappointing to hear this, but after carefully considering, I've concluded I can't provide you with the coaching you require at this time."*

It's an excellent approach to begin the topic if you do it that way, with your nuances.

This way, you don't hide anything, also at the same time, you don't talk about the big reveal. It conveys the message straight after preparing your customers to take it in the greatest possible manner.

- **Share why you decided to quit**

Once you have prepared the stage, take a moment to share why you are saying NO.

This is how I continued my discussion with *Susan - "I've come to the conclusion that I'm overcommitted after considering all of my responsibilities and how I might be of the most help. Now I've started conducting four webinars a week, which takes most of my time, and now I need to travel almost every week. Additionally, I recently began my YouTube engagement, and my leisure time should also be spent with my wife and family."*

Note: Keep in mind that details will differ from individual to individual. This is merely an example from my experience of recently cutting back on a few responsibilities.

It's crucial to be truthful at this stage in the discussion. The other person has a right to know your reasoning for withdrawing. **They may not want to know about every detail you will describe, but you still owe them a justification for your decision**.

Don't be too reserved here. Be clear and transparent.

Although you might believe that outlining your concerns will make the other person feel bad, having been on the receiving end of this talk, I can assure you that the effect is actually quite the contrary.

The higher the interpersonal cost of backing out increases, the more difficult it is for the other person to understand your intentions. Hence, share and express your intentions clearly why you are saying NO at the last moment.

In this case, the other person is obviously very important.

In some situations, your justifications need to be strong and specific, for example, informing your boss that you want to quit the project you have been recently assigned.

- **Say sorry if your audience deserves it**

Your audience may be due an apology depending on the consequences of your lack of commitment.

For instance, you should sincerely apologize to your best friend if you decide not to attend her wedding anniversary and she expects you to make it happen.

Similarly, you definitely owe your partner or boss a more sincere "sorry" if you have to cancel a planned vacation or can't complete a project you were supposed to finish. You should also provide sensible reasons for backing out because this will affect your future aspirations.

However, you don't need to apologize too much if you're skipping a vacation with some people you met at a wedding party a few weeks ago or if you're backing out of a task with coworkers you no longer trust. **Be friendly and kind, but don't punish yourself by apologizing for it**.

Saying, *"I'm sorry if I've disheartened you, and I hope this won't take you into too much trouble,"* is a kind attitude regardless of the situation. Being polite and sympathetic is a good strategy.

- **Try to find a way to contribute even when you are going to say NO**

Finding a means to be supportive even as you say NO is the most excellent apology. This one action can have a considerable impact on how a person takes your NO.

For instance, when I had to say NO to *Susan*, I suggested to her another life coach who I thought would be the best for her. She set up a meeting with him and found it promising and ideal for herself - even better than me.

You can see that I still get along well with *Susan* in this instance, as is evident.

The most effective approach to lessen the adverse effects of stepping out is to **find an alternative for yourself**. However, there are other methods to offer.

You can exchange ideas, information, tools, services, and recommendations.

From a distance, you can direct or assist the project or the other person. You can introduce the group to other potential aid-seekers and locations. When your availability increases, you can come back to the opportunity later.

Alternatively, you may support the project or your client in general and assist in any other possible way.

Before announcing the news about your NO, it's often a good idea to devise one or two specific ways to help the other person or the project you're leaving.

Your NO will be received much more amicably if you say, *"I know it's disappointing, and I really apologize for leaving for these reasons, but there's good news as well."* And then tell that good news.

I'm sure this approach may even be embraced!

People frequently fail to realize that even when you "displease" someone, you can still provide significant value for them. Seek out opportunities to help others on a proactive basis. And you might even develop a stronger bond with the participants than you would have if you had remained on board but put out only a half-hearted effort.

- **Stay connected, keep the relationship going, and continue to support the best possible way you can**

As we just saw, breaking a promise and keeping your relationships intact is possible. Make an effort to contact the individuals involved after you uncommit. Inquire about the status of the project or how that person is doing. Listen to their issues or any obstacles or gaps they may be facing. If possible, prepare a few introductions or solutions to those difficulties. Share information and tools wherever required. Offer advice and criticism when necessary.

Even if you cannot provide tangible assistance, expressing your moral support is essential. It has been more helpful to me to listen and support the other person during phone calls than to solve their problems.

Therefore, don't undervalue the impact of simply being there for someone after you've broken up with them.

Relationships are beautiful because they always come up with different prospects and aspirations. **A healthy relationship will endure minor setbacks like backing out of a promise after you've already said YES, provided it is well-maintained**. Before making any decisions, consider which ones would be best for the individuals you are associated with and yourself. That strategy will assist you in maintaining focus on the most important goal: **your relationship with that person**.

- **Saying NO should be one of your habits**

One of the most challenging things in life is to say NO, as we have discussed earlier. Being open about our abilities and interests goes against everything we have been taught from a young age. We are trained to be polite and strive to be team players. We don't want to cause a disturbance or annoy anyone.

Therefore, even if we know deep down that we want to say NO, we frequently say YES to things we can't or don't want to do.

Naturally, we only succeed in putting ourselves in a position where the costs of saying NO increase.

Then, when we realize at the end and want to back out, the disagreement and discomfort we tried so hard to avoid only get worse.

Or, if we realize it's too late to change our minds, we remain with the commitment, which causes us to feel unhappy, dissatisfied, and trapped. And we hardly ever show our best performance.

Saying NO before you've gone too far to quit is the key takeaway from this situation.

✓ But how do you decide whether to accept or decline an offer when it is offered to you?
✓ And if you do have to refuse someone, how can you do it before you get yourself into trouble?

Let me provide you a few tips here:

1. Take your time

Give yourself enough time before you commit to something. You must carefully weigh the pros and cons. It doesn't matter if you want to take a few hours or days (for small opportunities) or if you take even weeks or months (for more significant opportunities). Be really clear about the commitments you are going to commit.

Below are the sample questions you can ask yourself to gain clarity:

- What are you expecting from the other person?
- How do you define success?
- How much time and effort will be needed to take advantage of this opportunity?
- What benefits may you expect if you fulfill this commitment?
- What will you need to accomplish, alter, or get to meet your obligations?
- Do you believe you can (and wish to) fulfill their expectations? If yes, you are prepared and willing to meet this responsibility. Should the response be no, you now know what to do next.

2. Determine the hidden costs & consequences

- What would happen if your efforts failed to help the other person achieve the intended results?
- What would happen to your relationships, your image, and how you felt about yourself if you later broke this promise?
- Would breaking your commitment later harm your opportunities and possibilities for the future?
- How much involvement would be required from you?
- What would happen if I responded YES and later realized that I couldn't follow through on my commitment? Am I prepared to deal with that result? It might be worthwhile to participate if the answer is YES. However, if the reply is unquestionable NO, you must think twice before continuing.

3. Don't ignore the topsy-turvy in life

The majority of opportunities in life aren't clear-cut. Never accept a request that is certainly a success with no cost or assured to be a failure with no potential rewards.

Therefore, one of your tasks is to evaluate these many factors and give each one the appropriate weight.

For instance, the chance of damaging your relationships might not be that significant in a partnership with someone you don't have strong feelings for, on vacation with people you just met last night at a party, or at a job you want to quit shortly.

Each person's emotional gains and losses from saying YES are unique. One person finds incredible satisfaction and purpose in making their supervisors happy. While for others, spending time on a project or disappointing a coworker may not seem stressful or worrying.

Everybody is unique in their own way. Understanding who you are, how you behave under challenging circumstances, and what is most important to you would be best. More art than science is involved here. So, please give it a second look and be sure of it.

4. Finally, the time has come to communicate the message

The process for rejecting an offer or giving up an opportunity is similar to the one I discussed earlier.

The same rules hold true.

Explain the situation by saying that you gave the offer a considerable amount of thought, that you understand that they might be disappointed, but that you wish to be fair to everyone here.

Then, explain why you decided to say NO. Contrary to the script for saying NO after you've already said YES, here you only need to give a broad or high-level explanation of your motivations.

There are several good reasons to decline an offer right away, including - *"I'm already engaged to three other projects," "I'm planning for more vacations this year,"* and

"I promised myself that during the coming several months, I would devote more time to my family."

- **It's helpful when you become friendly with NO**

You'll become better at saying YES to the appropriate opportunities as you become more adept at communicating NO. Additionally, being choosier makes you better at the areas you commit to, which usually results in receiving more offers and possibilities.

I love this beautiful quote from **Warren Buffet** - *"We need to learn the slow YES and the quick NO."*

Maintain this awareness as you grow. It takes practice to develop the ability to turn down invites.

When opportunities come your way, keep making the time to thoughtfully analyze them, examine your benefits and drawbacks, and be willing to "upset" someone by saying NO!

When more people want to work with you, it could be alluring to start embracing every offer. High achievers frequently fall victim to the trap. However, ***the most prosperous people I've spoken with all emphasize how crucial it is to concentrate on small areas where they can perform exceptionally. And the only way to do it is to say NO quite often.***

I hope now you have a clear idea of how to say NO after you have already said YES, and why it is so important.

Let me conclude this learning with one of **Steve Jobs's** famous talks on **"Focusing is about saying NO."**

The talk goes like this:

"Apple suffered for several years from lousy engineering management, I have to say it. And there were people that were going off in eighteen different directions, doing arguably interesting things in each one of them. Good engineers! Lousy management!

And what happened was - you look at the farm that's been created with all these different animals going in different directions, and it doesn't add up. The total is less than the sum of the parts.

And, so we had to decide - what are the fundamental directions we're going in, and what makes sense and what doesn't. And there were a bunch of things that didn't. And microcosmically, they might have made sense; macrocosmically, they made no sense.

And you know the hardest thing is - when you think about focusing, you think focusing is saying YES!

No!

Focusing... is about saying NO! Focusing is about saying NO. And You've got to say no, no, no, no. And you say NO, you piss off people, and they go talk to the San Jose Mercury, and they write a shitty article about you.

Some of these people that have left, I know some of these people, they have done it in seven years, and you know they leave, and it's like the company's going to fall apart the next day. And so, you know, I think there'll be stories like that they come and go, ***but the focus is about saying NO, and the result of that focus is going to be some really great products where the total is much greater than the sum of the parts.****"*

10

Bonus Chapter: Powerful NOs For Life Mastery

Learning to say no is a skill that will benefit you throughout your entire life.

- Dale Carnegie

Although it's typically viewed as an adverse action, saying NO is actually a crucial tool for creating and upholding healthy boundaries in life. It gives us the authority to decide what we accept and keep out of our life. Whether in personal relationships, work, or social life, the ability to say NO can be the difference between feeling stressed and overwhelmed or being empowered and in control.

I'm delighted to provide real-life examples in this chapter of how to say NO in many situations.

I advise you to utilize these examples as a starting point and tweak them to match your particular requirements, even if they are meant to serve as a reference and source of inspiration.

While these examples can be helpful, it's vital to remember that there are other ways to say NO. Some examples might be more effective for you than others, or you might have your own unique manner of rejecting people. The crucial steps are discovering what works best for you and sticking with it.

Remember, saying NO takes courage, but it's a small step towards living a life of purpose and fulfillment.

So, buckle up, and let's dive into the empowering world of boundary setting!

#1) AT WORK

WHY:

Saying NO at work requires a delicate balance between being assertive and maintaining positive relationships with colleagues and superiors.

It is an essential tool to assert your priorities, boundaries, and capabilities, ensuring you do not become overwhelmed or overburdened with tasks beyond your capacity or outside of your job responsibilities.

By saying NO professionally and respectfully, you can avoid overextending yourself, preserve your mental and physical well-being, and maintain your ability to perform at your best.

Furthermore, declining tasks that are not in line with your skillset, goals, or job responsibilities can prevent disappointment and frustration for both - **the team** and **you**.

Additionally, saying NO when necessary reinforces personal credibility and integrity, as it shows that you are committed to delivering on your promises and commitments and can make well-informed decisions about your workload.

HOW:

- Thank you for considering me, but I don't think I'm the right fit for this project.
- I appreciate the offer, but I already have a full workload at the moment.
- I'm sorry, but I won't be able to take on any additional responsibilities at this time.
- Thank you for the invitation, but I won't be able to attend.
- I'm afraid I have to decline the request due to prior commitments.
- This doesn't fall under my job description. Please refer to our manager to learn who to ask.
- I appreciate the suggestion, but I prefer to focus on my current projects.
- Thank you for considering me, but I don't have the bandwidth to take on this project right now.

- I'm sorry, but I won't be able to provide the level of support you're looking for.
- I enjoyed helping you last time, but I am too busy to assist you right now.
- I appreciate the offer, but I don't think it aligns with my skillset.
- I'm afraid I won't be able to participate in this project, as I have other priorities at the moment.
- Unfortunately, I have too much to do today. I can help you another time.
- Now isn't a good time for me. I'll let you know if my schedule frees up.
- How about you try it on your own first, and then I can help you?
- I've actually changed my mind. I can no longer help you. Sorry for the inconvenience this may cause.
- I do not tolerate behavior that is unprofessional, disrespectful, or aggressive. I request that you treat me and others in the workplace with dignity and respect.
- I have noticed that your actions towards me and others are causing a negative impact in the workplace. I strongly encourage you to modify your behavior.

- I refuse to work in an environment where I am subjected to bullying or harassment. I am taking steps to address this issue and will no longer tolerate it.
- Bullying has no place in our workplace, and I will not be a part of it. I have notified our HR department about this issue.

#2) TO YOUR BOSS/MANAGER

WHY:

In some situations, you can refuse a request from your manager or employer. It is important to be aware of the consequences of saying NO and weigh them against the potential benefits it may bring.

By refusing, you may safeguard your interests and uphold your self-respect.

Saying NO is mainly done to advance one's own interests. Protecting your own time, health, or mental health may fall under this category.

For example, declining a manager's request to work overtime is acceptable if you already have other obligations. It may not be possible to fulfill the request without sacrificing other important commitments.

Saying NO can also help you safeguard your career. For example, you can protect your reputation by declining to do inappropriate, unethical, or illegal things.

You might feel insulted if you believe you are receiving unfair treatment or being exploited. Keep your dignity and respect by refusing to comply with such solicitations. It can also assist you in defending your own principles and convictions.

The potential repercussions of saying NO must be considered. Refusing could result in a damaged working relationship with your manager or boss or a poor performance review. Additionally, you might get passed up for promotions or other opportunities. It is essential to weigh these potential consequences against the potential benefits of saying NO.

HOW:

- I appreciate you considering me for this. I can work on it immediately if it's a top priority, but it will delay <<the project you're currently working on>> by 4 weeks.

- I'm not the right fit for this task. I can help you think of someone else to ask.

- Unfortunately, that's just not possible. It won't work out this time.

- Are you sure you want me to do that? I would rather not, but I appreciate you asking.

- This task doesn't align with my own principles. Could we change what I need to do?

- I appreciate the opportunity, but I already have several high-priority tasks on my plate.

- I told myself I wouldn't do that again. Thanks for respecting my decision.

- No, thank you. I would appreciate it if you accepted my choice.

- I appreciate your confidence in me, but I don't think I have the necessary skills for this project.

- Out of respect for my privacy, I hope you can understand my answer is NO.

- How about I help you with something else instead of me doing that?

- This doesn't seem like a healthy decision for me. I will have to regretfully decline.

- I'm afraid I won't be able to allocate the resources you're asking for now.

- I understand your request, but I don't think I can commit to it without compromising the quality of my work.

- I'm sorry, but I won't be able to meet the deadline you're requesting.

#3) TO YOUR FRIENDS

WHY:

Saying NO to a friend is acceptable since upholding sound boundaries is crucial for a satisfying friendship. It demonstrates respect for yourself and your needs when you say NO to a friend.

Additionally, it can aid in maintaining a more equal balance within the friendship and stop resentment from growing over time. It helps prevent burnout and overextending yourself.

You might experience tension and feel overwhelmed if you always say YES to every request or favor from a friend. You can protect your well-being and ensure you have the strength and resources to continue being a supportive friend by establishing boundaries and saying NO when required.

Saying NO can also facilitate better communication in the friendship. If you are constantly available and ready to say YES to your friends' all requests, they could not appreciate the significance of respecting your boundaries.

Having to say NO to a friend can also result in the creation of new relationships and experiences.

For example, you might have less time and energy for other pursuits and relationships if you continuously say YES to your friend. You can make more room for new experiences and relationships by establishing boundaries and using the word NO when appropriate.

HOW:

- Thanks for thinking of me, but I have other plans for that day.

- I appreciate the offer, but I can't commit to that right now.

- I hate to do this, but I won't be able to follow through on our plans.

- I wish I could, but I have prior obligations.

- That sounds fun, but I'm not available at that time.

- I wish I could assist, but I have other commitments that I need to prioritize.

- I'm sorry, I'm just not comfortable with that.

- I just found out I have an unexpected commitment that I need to attend to.

- I'd love to help, but I have too much on my plate at the moment.

- I'm sorry, I'm not feeling up to it today.

- I'd love to join you, but I need to take care of some things that day.

- Unfortunately, my circumstances have changed, and I won't be able to join you.

- Thanks for thinking of me, but I have some solo plans this time.

- I apologize, something came up, and I won't be able to make it.
- I'm sorry; I just realized I have a prior obligation that I can't reschedule.

#4) TO A JOB OFFER

WHY:

As a life coach, I have observed many people struggle to accept or reject a job offer. While it may be tempting to seize every opportunity, it's crucial to keep in mind that it's totally OK to turn down a job offer. In actuality, declining a job offer can be one of the best things you ever do for your career.

A mismatch between the job responsibilities and your talents and interests is one of the most significant justifications for rejecting a job offer. You could experience unhappiness and unfulfillment if you take a career that is not a good fit for your skills. Burnout can result from this, which will eventually harm your career.

The corporate culture is yet another justification for rejecting a job offer. You will likely not enjoy your job if you believe that the corporate culture conflicts with your principles or views. This may cause you to feel less satisfied and motivated at work, and it can even result in you leaving the company prematurely.

Mismatched values and skills aren't the only factors to consider; the salary and benefits package is also crucial. If the pay and benefits are insufficient, it might cause financial stress and harm your general well-being.

Although turning down a job offer can be challenging because of pay issues, it's crucial to remember that your ability to retain your financial security is essential to your long-term professional success.

It is also essential to consider the long-term career prospects of the role. It might not be the ideal decision for your career if the position does not provide opportunities for advancement. On the other hand, if the role offers the potential for career advancement and growth, it may be worth considering, even if the initial salary and benefits package is not ideal.

The commute should also be considered while considering whether to accept a job offer. A long commute can negatively impact your ability to balance work and life. It could be advisable to reject the job offer and hunt for one that is more accessible if the commute is too long or challenging.

Finally, it is vital to trust your instincts. You are likely correct if you have a gut feeling that the role is not suitable for you. Trusting your instincts can help you make the best decision for your career and well-being.

HOW:

- I appreciate the offer, but I have decided to pursue other opportunities.
- Thanks for considering me, but I have decided not to accept the offer at this time.
- I regret to say that I won't be able to accept the offer.
- I appreciate the opportunity, but I have decided to go in a different direction.
- Thanks for offering, but I have already accepted another position.
- I regret to say that the salary offered is not in line with industry standards.
- I'm sorry, but the job doesn't align with my career goals at this time.
- Thanks for the offer, but I need to decline due to personal circumstances.
- I'm grateful for the offer, but I am looking for a role that is more locally based and less focused on travel.
- I regret to say that the job location is not a good fit for my family.
- Thanks for the offer, but I have concerns about the company culture.
- I'm sorry, the compensation package is not what I was expecting.

- I regret that the job responsibilities do not match my skill set.

- Thanks for the offer, but I have a personal opportunity that I need to pursue.

- Thanks for considering me, but I have received a better offer from another company.

- I appreciate the offer, but I have concerns about the work-life balance.

- I regret to say that the commute is too far for me.

- I appreciate the opportunity, but I need to prioritize my earning potential in this role.

- I'm sorry, but the salary offered does not align with my qualifications and experience.

- I regret to say that I have had a change of heart and won't be able to join the company.

- Unfortunately, I have received a better offer that I need to accept.

- I apologize, but I have realized that the job is not a good fit for me after all.

- The position sounds exciting, but the requirement for frequent travel is not a good fit for me at this time.

#5) TO YOUR CLIENTS/CUSTOMERS

WHY:

Although it can be difficult, there are times when saying NO to clients and consumers is necessary to protect your time and resources.

If you consistently agree to every demand made by clients or customers, you can overwhelm yourself, resulting in burnout and reduced work quality. Overextending yourself can also lead to missed deadlines and broken promises, harming your credibility and reputation.

You can prioritize your work and concentrate on completing high-quality work for the clients and projects you have committed to by saying NO to clients and customers.

Moreover, saying NO to clients and customers can demonstrate your professionalism and assertiveness. By establishing clear limits and communicating your constraints, you show respect for yourself, and your time and a willingness to stand up for what is best for your business and yourself.

Customers and clients will value your honesty and integrity, which can help you earn their respect and trust.

In conclusion, it can be uncomfortable to say NO to clients and consumers, but it's necessary to manage a successful business. You may guarantee the expansion and survival of your company while preserving positive connections with your clients and consumers by guarding your time and resources, acting professionally, and establishing clear boundaries.

HOW:

- I understand this is important to you, but I must decline this request. However, I would be happy to help you find another solution.
- I understand your request, but I cannot fulfill it now.
- Unfortunately, that is outside of the scope of our agreement/services.
- I'm sorry, but I won't be able to accommodate that request as it goes beyond our agreed services.
- Thank you for reaching out, but I am unable to fulfill that particular request.
- I understand the importance of your request, but I cannot comply with it as it is beyond the scope of what we offer.
- I appreciate your understanding that we have certain policies and limitations that prevent us from fulfilling that request.
- I understand the importance of your request, but I cannot comply with it at this time.
- I apologize, but due to our current workload, we are unable to take on additional requests at this time.

- I apologize for the confusion, but I must retract my previous commitment. I will not be able to fulfill the request as initially agreed.

- I regret to inform you that due to unforeseen circumstances, I must change my previous decision, and I will not be able to fulfill the request.

- I'm sorry for any inconvenience, but I have had a change of circumstances, and I will not be able to deliver on my previous commitment.

- I understand that you have a deadline, but I cannot be pressured into making a decision that is not in the best interest of both of us.

- I appreciate your urgency, but I cannot compromise my standards or make exceptions for aggressive behavior.

- I understand your frustration, but I will not be intimidated or pressured into making a decision.

- I regret your dissatisfaction, but I will not respond to aggressive behavior. Let's discuss this matter calmly and respectfully.

- I appreciate your interest, but I cannot allow aggressive behavior to dictate the terms of our interaction.

- I appreciate your business, but the fee you offer does not accurately reflect the value of our services.

- I regret to say that the proposed fee is not in line with the industry standards for the scope of work.
- I understand you have limited funds, but the fee you offer is insufficient to complete the project to the quality we promise.

#6) TO YOUR PARENTS/PARENTS-IN-LAW

WHY:

It might be challenging to refuse requests from parents and in-laws, but occasionally doing so promotes growth in one's self and relationships.

Even though family connections are frequently emotional and complicated, it's crucial to establish healthy boundaries and have open honest communication. Saying NO to your parents and parents-in-law might help you maintain your independence and avoid burnout.

For instance, saying NO to requests for help or obligations to attend events can help prioritize self-care and reduce stress.

While it may be tempting to constantly agree to the requests of parents and parents-in-law, it is essential to set boundaries and prioritize one's own mental and emotional well-being. It can also help keep tensions and animosity in the relationship at bay.

Saying NO to your parents and parents-in-law can also signify maturity and independence.

You demonstrate independence and respect for your needs and values by defending yourself and establishing firm limits. As it promotes courteous and open communication, this can aid in developing healthier and more equitable family connections.

HOW:

- I am grateful for your support, but I must follow my own path.

- I understand your perspective, but I am ready to take responsibility for my own life.

- I understand your position, but I must learn from my experiences.

- I respect your guidance, but I have to make my own mistakes.

- I understand where you're coming from, but I have made up my mind on this.

- I respect your opinion, but I have a different perspective on this.

- I understand your point of view, but I have to make decisions that are best for me.

- Thank you for understanding. I believe I should say NO to this request at this time.

- I need some time to consider your request and devise a solution that works for both of us.

- I need some time to think about it and get back to you.
- I don't feel comfortable with that, and I need to stick to my boundaries.
- I appreciate your suggestion, but I have thought it through and don't think it's the right choice for me.
- I'm sorry, but my schedule is hectic at the moment, and I won't be able to accommodate a visit.
- I think it's best to reschedule for later when it's more convenient for both of us.
- I'm sorry, but the timing just isn't right for a visit. Let's plan for another time.
- I think it's best to have a transparent and open conversation about our expectations and boundaries.
- I appreciate your offer, but I have to respectfully say NO.
- I understand your financial situation, but I'm not in a position to provide financial support right now.
- I'm sorry, but I don't feel comfortable lending money at this time.
- I appreciate your understanding, but I have to say no to your request for financial support.

- I appreciate the invitation, but I already have plans for that evening.
- I'm sorry, but I have a prior commitment that I can't reschedule.
- I'm sorry, but I don't feel comfortable doing what you're asking due to social pressure.
- I think it's important for me to stand up for myself and not give in to social pressure.

#7) TO YOUR CHILDREN

WHY:

Parenting requires you to learn how to say NO to your child. It is a means to establish limits, instill accountability, and promote independence. Even though it might seem counterintuitive, telling your child NO is a display of affection and concern.

For children to grow up to be well-rounded, responsible individuals, they require structure and direction. Saying NO helps them understand what is expected of them and acceptable behavior.

Saying NO is also a way to protect your child.

For example, if they want to stay up late, overeat junk food, or engage in dangerous activities, it is your job as a parent to step in and set limits. Saying NO in these situations is not a punishment but a way to ensure their safety and well-being.

Saying NO can also aid children in developing resilience. They develop coping mechanisms and adaptability when faced with disappointment or dissatisfaction. This helps them develop coping mechanisms that they will use throughout their lives.

It has been observed in various studies that children who are never allowed to feel dissatisfaction or disappointment may struggle later in life when they encounter challenges and disappointments.

Children learn about responsibility by hearing NO.

Setting limits and upholding them teaches kids that their actions have repercussions. They begin to realize how their actions affect themselves and those around them. This teaches kids to accept accountability for their actions and helps them feel responsible.

It's critical to keep in mind that you must provide your child with an explanation when you say NO.

Children may find it frustrating and puzzling when parents simply say NO without providing any explanation. They could feel as though they are being unfairly punished and wonder why they aren't allowed to do something.

By allowing your child to ask questions and gain insight from experience, you assist them in understanding your decision by explaining why you are saying NO.

Remember, refusing anything does not mean you are being rigid or inflexible. It is essential to be open to negotiation and compromise.

Children need to feel that they have some agency and control over their own lives and understand that there are rules and limitations.

Being open to negotiation can help your child learn the art of compromise and the importance of finding solutions that work for everyone involved.

HOW:

- I understand that you want to do that, but it's not possible right now.
- I think it's essential for you to understand why I am saying NO.
- I'm sorry, but that's not something that fits within our family rules and expectations.
- I appreciate your perspective, but I must first put your long-term interests.
- I think it's best if we find a compromise or alternative solution.
- I believe it is essential for you to understand the value of money and saving.

- I appreciate your request, but we have to make the decision that we believe is best for our family's financial stability.

- I understand you want that, but we can't afford it right now.

- I understand your perspective, but I must prioritize other responsibilities and commitments.

- I'm sorry, but something has come up, and I can't fulfill that promise.

- I think it's important for you to understand that sometimes plans can change.

- I understand that you need money, but we have a budget that we need to stick to.

- I understand you want that, but it's not good for you right now.

- Unfortunately, my answer is still NO.

- That's a hard NO from me.

- I understand you want sweets, but it's not good for you to have them all the time.

- I know you're craving something sweet, but let's have something healthy first. Maybe an apple?

- I understand that you want to go play, but exams are coming up, and it's important to focus on your studies.

- I think it's important for you to understand why it's necessary to focus on your studies right now.

- I appreciate your understanding, but I have to decline your request to go play at this time.

- I understand you want to stay up late, but bedtime is a non-negotiable boundary for a good night's sleep.

- I understand you want to stay up late, but I have to say NO because it could negatively impact your physical and mental health.

- I'm sorry, but I must set clear expectations for completing homework and household chores before playtime.

- I think it's important for you to understand the importance of being respectful and following rules.

- I know you want the latest toy, but learning how to make responsible decisions with your money is important.

- I'm sorry, but I have to decline your request to participate in that activity because it's unsafe.

- I understand you want to try that food, but I have to say NO because it could harm your health.

#8) IN PERSONAL RELATIONSHIPS

WHY:

Learning to say NO is essential in personal relationships to uphold healthy boundaries and safeguard your well-being. It is crucial to realize that declining requests, invites, or demands that conflict with your principles, requirements, or wants is entirely appropriate.

Saying NO is **a method to express your autonomy and ensure that your demands and priorities are considered, not an indication of being self-centered or rude**.

People can sustain happy, lasting relationships built on respect and understanding by having clear limits. In personal relationships, saying NO helps to establish clear and healthy boundaries. When you can say NO to requests or demands that are unreasonable or uncomfortable, you are sending a message about what is acceptable and what is not. By doing so, misunderstandings and disagreements can be avoided, and relationships can stay healthy.

You are taking care of yourself and ensuring that you are not overextended or taken advantage of by saying NO to unreasonable demands that conflict with your principles. This helps maintain a healthy balance between giving and receiving, preventing you from feeling drained or exhausted.

Saying NO can also **strengthen relationships**.

When you can assert your boundaries and say NO when necessary, you communicate that you respect yourself and take your needs and desires seriously.

As a result, you can better recognize each other as independent beings deserving of respect, which deepens your relationship and helps to foster trust. The relationship may suffer when people can't say NO in intimate relationships.

Remember that it's not always simple to say NO in personal relationships. Setting boundaries can be challenging, particularly when interacting with persistent or demanding people. However, saying NO can get more manageable and natural with time and effort. Expressing NO firmly and politely is equally essential to avoid misunderstandings and conflicts.

HOW:

- I appreciate the offer, but I need to prioritize my own well-being and say NO.
- I understand you need help, but I'm currently overwhelmed and need to focus on myself. So I'll have to say NO this time.
- I can't commit to that right now. I need to take care of myself and ensure I have the energy and resources to maintain my health.
- I'm sorry, but I must set boundaries and prioritize my needs. So I'll have to say NO to that request.
- I value our relationship, but I need to prioritize my own well-being. So I'll have to respectfully decline your offer and say NO.

- I understand that you have a different perspective, but I need to ensure that I keep my boundaries in place for my well-being. So I'll have to say NO this time.

- I understand you would like me to <<insert request>>, but I need to maintain my personal boundaries and say NO.

- I don't think that's a good fit for me at this time.

- I'm flattered that you thought of me, but I don't think it's a good fit for me at this time. I have an important meeting tomorrow and need to be well rested. I don't want to compromise my responsibilities for a night out.

- I'm grateful for the invitation, but I don't think it's a good fit for me at this time. I have other commitments that take up most of my time and energy, and I don't want to spread myself too thin. Maybe I can join in the future if my schedule opens up.

- I appreciate the offer, but I don't think it's a good fit for me at this time. I have no need for this product right now, and I don't want to make an unnecessary purchase. Thank you for understanding.

- I understand that you would like me to attend the party, but I won't be able to make it this time. I appreciate the invitation, though.

- I need some alone time to recharge; I won't be able to hang out today.

- I appreciate the offer to lend me money, but I've decided to work on improving my financial habits, so I need to decline.

- I cannot go on a trip this weekend, but maybe we can plan for a different time when it works better for both of us.

- I've thought about it, and my answer is still NO. I hope you can understand and respect my decision.

- I can't do that today, but how about we do it tomorrow instead?

- I am not comfortable with that, but let's find a different solution that works for us.

- I would love to go out to dinner with you tonight, but I have a big project due tomorrow that I need to finish. Can we do it next week instead?

- I understand that you want to go camping for the weekend, but I'm not comfortable being that far away from home. How about we plan a day trip to a nearby park instead?

- I appreciate your offer to help with the renovation project, but I need some time to work on it. Maybe we can talk about it again in a few weeks.

- I appreciate that you want to make plans for the holiday, but I need time to think about what I want to do. Can we talk about it later in the week?

- I understand that you enjoy bungee jumping, but it's just not something I'm interested in. Let's find something else that we both enjoy doing.

#9) TO A MARRIAGE PROPOSAL

WHY:

Saying NO to a marriage proposal can be difficult, but it is essential to remember that it is okay to decline an offer if it does not feel right.

There are several reasons to reject a proposal, and each person will have their own justifications. For instance, a person can feel unprepared to commit to a lifelong relationship, or they might not feel fascinated with the person who has proposed.

Additionally, practical considerations may make a marriage unwise, such as differences in values, goals, or lifestyle, or a lack of compatibility in areas such as religion, politics, or finances.

It's also possible for someone to reject a proposal because they want more time to get to know the other person before committing or because they are unsure about the relationship. This is an excellent reason to say NO to a proposal. Remember that mutual trust and understanding are the foundation of a strong relationship. It would be best to wait until these elements are in place before committing to something long-term.

Regardless of the reasons for rejection, **it is essential to do it politely and respectfully. This entails taking the time to have an in-depth discussion with the individual who made the proposal, being open and honest, and being transparent about why the proposal is being rejected**.

Although having this conversation can be challenging, **it's essential to do so with sensitivity, understanding, and honesty regarding one's sentiments and concerns**.

Rejecting a proposal sometimes presents a chance for development and introspection.

Consider your personal goals, values, desires, and the kind of relationship and partnership you want to have in the future.

When declining a marriage proposal, there is no right or wrong decision; it is a personal choice. The decision must be taken with care for both people involved and must be done so in an open, sincere, and respectful manner.

It is okay to reject a proposal if it does not seem right. There is always the chance for growth, self-reflection, and fresh beginnings, regardless of whether the decision is made for practical, emotional, or personal reasons.

HOW:

- I appreciate your proposal and the effort you have put into it, but I'm not ready for marriage now. I need more time to think about what I want for my future.

- I appreciate your proposal, but this just doesn't feel like the right time for me. I need to focus on my career and personal growth right now.

- I know this is not what you were hoping to hear, but I want you to know that I care about and respect you. I hope we can still be close friends.

- I appreciate your proposal, but I have personal and financial goals that I need to achieve before I can consider marriage. I hope you can understand and respect my decision.

- I am not ready for marriage yet, but I would love to continue our relationship and see where it goes. How about we take things slow and see where it leads us?

- I respect your offer, but I need more time to think about it. Can we talk about it again in a few months?

- Can we talk in private? I have something important I want to discuss with you.

- I appreciate your proposal, but I'm not ready for that level of commitment. I need more time to figure out what I want in life.

- I'm sorry, but I don't see a future together. I don't think we have the same life values and goals.

- I'm sorry, but I need to end our relationship. I don't see a future for us together, and I think it's best if we go our separate ways.

- I'm grateful for your offer, but I need to be single for a while. I need time to focus on myself and figure out what I want in life.

- I highly regard your proposal, but I don't believe in marriage. I don't think it's the right path for me, and I hope you can understand and respect my decision.

- I want to continue our relationship and spend more time together, but I think it would be best if we wait until I am in a better financial position before we take the next step.

- I'm here if you need to talk, but I understand if you need some time and space to process this. Let me know if you'd like to talk.

- I can't marry you because I don't think it's right for me at this point in my life. I have other goals and ambitions that must be explored before considering such an important commitment.

#10) TO YOUR LOVED ONES WHEN THEY ARE ASKING FOR MONEY

WHY:

A person may deny a request for money for various reasons, such as a lack of financial means, conflicting demands, or the need to preserve healthy relationships.

One of the most common reasons for declining a request for money from close friends or family members is a lack of personal resources. This can include limited funds, high levels of debt, or other financial obligations.

If you are struggling to meet your financial needs, providing financial assistance to others may not be possible. In these cases, it is essential to prioritize your financial stability and decline the request for money.

If you have concerns that your friend will not repay the loan, it is perfectly acceptable to decline the request. Rejecting him does not mean that you are a bad friend; it simply shows that you are responsible and aware of your financial boundaries.

Conflicting priorities are another reason for declining a request for money from close friends or family members. Everyone has different responsibilities and obligations, and balancing these with requests for financial assistance is essential.

For instance, you cannot help others financially because you have bills, debts, or other financial commitments that must be paid.

Saying NO to close friends or family members when they are asking for money can also be necessary for maintaining healthy relationships. Providing financial assistance to others can be generous but can also create expectations and obligations that strain relationships.

If you are repeatedly asked for financial assistance or feel that your generosity is being taken for granted, it may be necessary to decline requests for money to maintain healthy relationships.

Saying NO to close friends or family members when they ask for money does not necessarily mean ending the relationship. Relationships are built on trust, respect, and mutual support, and saying NO to a request for money can be an opportunity to strengthen these qualities.

By communicating clearly and respectfully and offering alternative forms of support, close friends or family members can continue to build and maintain strong relationships, even if you cannot provide financial assistance.

HOW:

- I understand why you are asking, and I wish I could give you the money, but unfortunately, I cannot afford it right now.

- I'm sorry, but I'm not in a place right now where I can give you the money you need. I hope you understand.

- I appreciate your request, but giving money is not something I'm able to do right now. I'm sorry.

- I understand that you're in a tough spot, but I just don't have the resources to help you at this time.

- I know it's a difficult situation, but I don't have the money to lend right now.

- I wish I could offer you financial assistance, but I just don't have the resources to do so. I hope you understand.

- I need a bit more time to think this over. Can I get back to you on Monday?

- I understand you need money, but I cannot give you a loan now. However, I know a credit counselor who could offer you some financial advice. Would you be interested in her contact information?

- I wish I could help, but right now, I have to focus on paying off my own debts and saving for the future.

- I understand that you're in a difficult situation, and I wish I could help. Unfortunately, I am unable to provide any money right now. Is there anyone else you could reach out to or anything else I could help you with?

- Thank you for thinking of me, but I'm afraid I won't be able to help financially. I'd still be happy to provide emotional support if you need it.

- I can't give you money right now, but I'm willing to help you in other ways. Can I help you create a budget or look for ways to save money?

- I understand you need money, but I can't give it to you now. I'm happy to help you find a job or other ways to make money, but I won't be able to provide you with any money.

- I'm sorry, but I cannot give you money right now. I know this isn't the answer you were hoping for, but I need to be responsible with my finances. Can I help you find other ways to get the money you need?

- I'm sorry, but I have a policy of not lending money to family members because it can cause strain on relationships; I hope you understand. Maybe there are alternative solutions we can explore together?

- I appreciate you thinking of me and asking for help, but I have made a conscious decision to not lend money to friends or family. I don't want to put our relationship at risk, and I hope you can understand my position.

- I'm sorry, but lending money to the family can be complicated, and I prefer to avoid it. Let's see if there's something else I can do to help.

- Dad, I know you're in a tough spot, but I've been working hard to get my own finances in order. Lending you money would set me back, and I just can't afford to do that right now.

- I hear you and understand how important this is, but I can't afford to lend you money right now. I have my own financial obligations, and I need to ensure I'm taking care of myself before I can help others.

- Dad, I wish I could give you the money, but I'm just not in a place to do that right now. My financial situation is tight, and I must focus on taking care of myself first.

#11) TO VOLUNTEER & PROVIDE COMMUNITY SERVICES

WHY:

You may turn down a volunteer opportunity or a request for community services for various reasons, such as a lack of personal resources, conflicting priorities, or the need to look after your own well-being.

Lack of personal resources is among the most frequent reasons for rejecting volunteer opportunities or requests for community assistance. Time, effort, and money are all examples of resources.

Contributing to the community and volunteering can be stressful and time- and energy-intensive, which may not be possible for everyone. Additionally, some people might not have the financial means to support volunteer work or projects that contribute to the community, such as paying for transportation or materials. When making this choice, it's critical to put one's own well-being and financial security first.

Conflicting priorities are another reason to say NO to volunteering and performing community tasks.

For instance, someone might not be able to volunteer because of their demanding work schedule, family obligations, or other commitments. In this situation, you must put your personal needs and obligations first and turn down the chance to volunteer or offer community activities.

Volunteering and providing community services can be rewarding experiences, but they can also be physically, emotionally, and mentally demanding. If you are struggling with your own well-being or experiencing stress or burnout, taking a break from volunteering and community services may be necessary to focus on your needs.

Remember that volunteering and providing community services are not the only ways to positively impact the world. There are many other ways to contribute, such as supporting local organizations, making financial donations, or advocating for important causes. Even if a person is unable or unwilling to donate their time or offer their services to the community, they can still have a beneficial influence in other ways.

HOW:

- I appreciate the opportunity, but I'm afraid I won't be able to help this time. My schedule is already full, and I need to focus on other commitments.

- I'm sorry, but I cannot offer financial support or volunteer time now. I hope you can understand.

- I'm afraid I won't be able to contribute, but I've donated to another organization that aligns with my values.

- I wish I could assist, but I now have prior obligations. Perhaps I could recommend someone else who might be available to help out.

- I appreciate the offer, but volunteering and community service are not my areas of expertise or interest. I need to focus on what I am passionate about.

- I'd love to help in the future, but I have a lot on my plate right now. Can we touch base in a few months to see if my schedule has opened up?

- Thank you for considering me, but I need to decline this opportunity. I appreciate the offer and the chance to support the community in other ways.

- I appreciate the opportunity to support you, but I cannot contribute now.

- I am sorry, but I have other commitments that I need to focus on right now.

- I cannot support charities at the moment due to my circumstances.

- I regret to inform you that I cannot contribute or volunteer my time.

- I have already committed to another organization and must prioritize that.

- I wish I could help, but I have to decline due to current constraints.

- I'm afraid I have to decline, but I will keep your organization in mind for future support.

- I cannot commit to volunteering or donating now, but I wish the cause the best of luck.

- I cannot offer my support for this charity or volunteer opportunity, but thank you for thinking of me.

- I'm sorry, but I have to decline as I'm focusing on supporting local organizations and causes in my community.

- I cannot contribute financially, but I've found alternative ways to support the cause, such as participating in fundraising events.

- I'm unable to donate due to unexpected personal expenses, but I hope to be able to support the cause in the future.

#12) TO RESIST SOCIAL PRESSURE TO CONFORM

WHY:

It can be challenging to reject society's expectations and norms, but it's crucial to remember that putting your values and well-being first is acceptable.

Conforming to social conventions frequently results in giving up your ideals and aspirations, leaving you feeling disconnected and unhappy.

One of the most common reasons for feeling pressure to conform to societal norms is a desire for acceptance and belonging. People often want to fit in with their peers and be accepted by their communities, which can lead to pressure to conform to societal norms.

However, it is important to remember that acceptance and belonging come from being true to oneself and surrounding oneself with people who appreciate and respect one's unique qualities and beliefs.

Another reason why it is okay to say NO when feeling the pressure to conform to societal norms is to **maintain your own sense of identity and authenticity**.

Following social conventions can frequently result in a loss of identity and a sense of separation from your own values and ideas. By resisting the pressure to conform and staying true to yourself, you can maintain a sense of self and live a life consistent with your values and goals.

HOW:

- Thanks for thinking of me, but I think I'll pass on being a superhero for now.

- I appreciate the offer, but I don't feel comfortable doing that. Thank you for understanding.

- I have to decline the invitation, but my friend will happily join you.

- I won't be able to work that shift; I need some time to take care of myself.

- I'm sorry, but I don't support that cause, and I won't be able to participate.

- Can I get back to you on that? I need to think it over first.

- I won't be able to attend all social events from now on; I need to focus on my studies.

- I can't make it to the party, but I'd be happy to hang out with you another time.

- I understand it's the norm to work long hours, but I value my work-life balance. I won't be able to work overtime this time.

- I appreciate the invitation, but I don't drink alcohol. I'll have a non-alcoholic beverage instead.

- I know it's expected to attend every social event, but I need to prioritize my mental health and take a break this weekend.

- I'm flattered that you think I'd be a good fit for the project, but I don't want to take on more work right now. I need to focus on my current responsibilities.

- I'm aware that it's common to conform to fashion trends, but I prefer to dress in a way that makes me comfortable and reflects my personal style.

- I know it's popular to participate in extreme sports, but I prefer to stick to less dangerous activities.

- I understand it's the norm to own a car, but I choose to use public transportation or a bike instead.

- I'm aware that it's expected to spend a lot of money on gifts for special occasions, but I'd instead save my money or give a thoughtful, handmade gift.

- I appreciate the offer to join the committee, but I need to focus on my projects and responsibilities at this moment.

- I know it's common to eat meat at every meal, but I've chosen to follow a vegetarian diet.

- I understand it's the norm to take a certain career path, but I want to pursue a different route that aligns more with my passions and interests.

- I'm aware it's popular to keep up with the latest technology, but I prefer to limit my screen time and focus on other activities.

- I appreciate the invitation to go out on the weekend, but I must prioritize rest and self-care.

- I know it's expected to conform to certain beauty standards, but I embrace my natural appearance and focus on inner beauty.

- I understand it's the norm to celebrate holidays in a certain way, but I prefer to create my own traditions that align with my values and beliefs.

In conclusion, with this chapter, I have provided comprehensive information on effectively communicating a NO in various aspects of life.

I believe this **bonus chapter** should be a valuable tool for you to assert your boundaries and make decisions that align with your values and goals. By understanding different approaches to saying NO, you can choose the best strategy for you in any situation, whether in a professional or personal setting.

I hope this information will empower you to confidently and respectfully decline invitations or requests that do not align with your priorities.

Good luck!

Conclusion

The art of saying **NO** is a complex and multi-faceted concept, requiring insight into its psychological and practical components.

This book explored the various aspects of saying NO, from **the role of limiting beliefs** and **setting boundaries to self-esteem and confidence**. Additionally, we looked at the concept of the **"18th Camel,"** or the underlying **reasoning behind the decision**, and how to utilize techniques to **communicate our refusal effectively**.

We also learned that **the ability to say NO is an essential part of life**, allowing us to prioritize our values and goals and say YES to the things that matter the most. However, the fear and guilt associated with saying NO can make us hesitant to assert ourselves and stand up for what we believe in.

We saw that **confidence and self-esteem are critical components of saying NO**. A strong sense of self-worth and belief in our abilities can help us express our boundaries and overcome limiting beliefs. Alternatively, **a lack of self-esteem can make it difficult to assert ourselves and stand up for our values**.

Furthermore, we discussed the importance of saying NO even after saying YES. It is possible to have agreed to something without being aware of the implications or considering our own needs. Thus, **it is essential to take our decisions and YES into account and have the courage to decline if necessary**. Doing so can protect our relationships and prevent us from overextending ourselves.

Ultimately, we found -

Understanding the psychological and practical techniques of saying NO can help us build healthier relationships and a more rewarding life. We can gain the strength to confidently say NO, stand up for our beliefs, and live a life in line with our values and aspirations.

I hope you have taken away valuable lessons from this book, which may be applied to your personal and professional life.

Arigato,

Ravi L Tewari

MAY I BE THE CHANNEL OF BLESSINGS FOR SOMEONE TODAY!

References

Understanding the art of saying NO can be challenging to master; however, my knowledge and understanding of it come from my life experiences and studies of various books and websites. While it is impossible to cite all of them, some of the beneficial resources I consulted include:

- www.betterup.com
- www.clockify.me
- www.crosswalk.com
- www.exploringyourmind.com
- www.forbes.com
- www.hbr.org
- www.indeed.com
- www.jordanharbinger.com
- www.linkedin.com
- www.marieforleo.com
- www.pon.harvard.edu
- www.psychcentral.com
- www.ted.com
- www.theswaddle.com
- www.tinybuddha.com
- www.wikihow.com
- https://www.youtube.com/watch?v=-iUag3c9HRc
- https://www.youtube.com/watch?v=FtPRrn5nwAo
- https://www.youtube.com/watch?v=H8eP99neOVs
- https://www.youtube.com/watch?v=qwzPJhutVaY

Disclaimer

This book is for entertainment purposes only. Readers acknowledge that the author does not render legal, financial, medical, or professional advice. The content within this book has been derived from various sources. Please consult a licensed professional before attempting any techniques outlined in this book.

By reading this document, the reader agrees that under no circumstances is the author responsible for any direct or indirect losses incurred as a result of the use of the information contained within this document, including but not limited to errors, omissions, or inaccuracies. Adherence to all applicable laws and regulations, including international, federal, state, and local governing professional licensing, business practices, advertising, and all other jurisdiction, is the sole responsibility of the purchaser or reader. Neither the author nor the publisher assumes any responsibility or liability whatsoever on behalf of the purchaser or reader of these materials. Any perceived slight of any individual or organization is purely unintentional.

About The Author

Ravi Tewari is a bestselling author in the field of **self-help & development and a life coach, mentor, and motivational speaker**.

Visit https://neelamravi.com/freegift to access ***"31 Most Powerful Thoughts For The Day To Bring Self-Transformation In You"*** for **FREE**.

Ravi started his career as a software developer at Wipro Technologies, and now after 12 years of IT experience, he is the **founder & CEO of IoT Meeting Hub™**.

He is a **certified Ho'oponopono, EFT, and Crystal healer** as well. He loves to conduct workshops and webinars to teach people about these ancient and profound techniques. His motivational classes & speeches are solely based on his own experiences and learnings that inspire many people to live a more rewarding and fulfilling life. ***He believes in sharing knowledge and giving 10x values.***

In his books, Ravi shares over 12 years of practical knowledge and the profound wisdom he gained early on about resilience, resourcefulness, self-discovery, and self-management. He believes in turning life lessons into actionable steps and developing a healthy relationship with yourself, others, and life itself.

Other books Ravi has written:

- The Art of Saying NO
- Immediate Action
- manifest WEALTH & ABUNDANCE as you read
- from NIGHT-OWL to MORNING-LARK
- SELF-MOTIVATION like CRAZY
- GRATITUDE - LET THE UNIVERSE DO ITS MAGIC

You can contact him at: ravi@neelamravi.com

Or visit: https://neelamravi.com/ravi

Scan the below QR code to explore more of his books:

May I Ask You For A Small Favor?

At the outset, I want to give you a big thanks for reading this book. You could have chosen any other book, but you took mine, and I appreciate this.

I hope you have at least a few actionable insights that will positively impact your daily life.

Can I ask for 30 seconds more of your time?

I'd love it if you could leave a review of the book. That will help me grow my readership by encouraging folks to take a chance on my books.

Keeping it straight - reviews are the lifeblood of any author.

It will take less than a minute of your time but will tremendously help me reach out to more people.

Please consider leaving an honest review on your favorite store if you enjoyed this book. And I'd love to see your review. Thanks for your support.

MAY I BE THE CHANNEL OF BLESSINGS FOR SOMEONE TODAY!

Preview Of The Book: Immediate Action

-- Start of Preview --

I remember an exciting story based on a frog's behavior toward procrastination. Here it goes. I hope you will like it.

The story -

Once, a frog was put into a vessel of water. The water temperature was raised higher to some extent. The frog did not try to jump out of the vessel and procrastinated the thought of jumping out. It just stayed there because it could adjust its body temperature accordingly.

The frog keeps on adapting to the increase in temperature. Finally, when the water temperature was raised to the boiling point, the frog couldn't adjust its body temperature to the extreme boiling point, so it finally decided to jump out of the vessel.

But unfortunately, the frog could not jump out of the vessel because it had lost all its strength in adjusting its temperature. When it decided to jump out, it was too late. Very soon, eventually, the frog died inside the vessel.

The question -

What was the real reason the frog couldn't jump out of the vessel? Will you blame the frog or the hot water for it?

Moral -

The frog couldn't make it due to its procrastination - its own inability to decide when it had to jump out. In life, we all need to adjust according to the situation. Procrastination may lead to severe consequences. Of course, there may be occasions when we must face the problem, but we should take the appropriate action when we have the strength to do so before it's too late. ***We must walk out before we need to jump.***

Good or bad?

I'm sure you must know the literal meaning of procrastination. Procrastination is the action of unnecessarily and voluntarily delaying or postponing something despite knowing that there will be negative consequences for doing so.

The word originated from the Latin word ***procrastinatus,*** *which evolved from the prefix* ***pro-****, meaning* ***"forward,"*** *and* ***crastinus,*** *meaning* ***"of tomorrow."***

Let me put it in even more simple words -

Procrastination is the inability to complete a task even if you know you should. It is a phenomenon that everyone experiences, including the world's most successful individuals, so there is no need to feel ashamed of it. So, the objective is to handle it well rather than try to remove it, which would be impossible.

The human mind understands that it is a common experience involving delays in everyday chores. We sometimes even put off salient tasks such as meeting our doctors for regular check-ups, attending appointments, submitting status reports or academic assignments, or even initiating a stressful issue with our partner! Generally, it is thought of as habitual human behavior.

So,

- *Is it normal to procrastinate?*
- *Is procrastination really a problem or habit?*
- *Is procrastination good or bad?*
- *Should we live with this or stay away from it?*
- *Some people love delaying their regular tasks, while others are strict about following their schedules. So, which one is better?*

If you also have such doubts in your mind, congratulations! You have the right book in your hands! This will clear all your procrastination questions and provide you many solutions to deal with it in any situation in your life.

I'm not going to say whether procrastination is good or bad at this right moment. But I promise to give a fulfilling answer as you continue to read this book. Let me procrastinate my answer as of now :-).

There is a reason behind delaying my answer about procrastination. I never suggest you accept or reject ***"the facts"*** *blindly because people say so or social media shows so. Everything has two sides to the coin, and it's not wise to accept or agree to only a single side.*

If you think procrastination is not good, why do researchers say that ***sometimes moderate procrastination is a must because it gives your brain time to think deeply over a task or problem and creates space for greater creativity, innovations, and new ideas?***

And if you say procrastination is good, then ***why do research data show that procrastination harms our work, relationships, career, and overall health? Why do students who procrastinate experience higher frustration, stress, and anxiety levels? Why sometimes does it lead to severe issues like low self-esteem and depression?***

So, considering all the above aspects, it's too early to decide about procrastination. But, believe me, as you go through this book and read every chapter, you will gain more insights about procrastination. For the time being, let's procrastinate your opinion about procrastination :-).

Whatever your opinion is about procrastination, let's see what **Bill Gate,** *a co-founder of Microsoft, said once during an interview about it -*

"I had one habit that I developed when I was at college. That was actually a very bad habit, which was I like to show people that I didn't do any work. And that I didn't go to classes and I didn't care. And that the very last minute, like two days before the test, I'd get serious about it. And people thought that was funny. Then when I went into business, that was a really bad habit. And it took me a couple of years to get over that. Nobody praised me because I would do things at the last minute. Procrastination is not a good habit."

And here is what the **Bhagavad Gita,** *a 700-verse Hindu scripture that is part of the epic Mahabharata, says about procrastination -*

"Procrastination is seen when we are influenced by **Tamo Guna** *(the quality in the universe that obscures higher consciousness and the unity of life.). When* **Gita** *says that we are influenced by* **Gunas** *(a concept in Hinduism and Sikhism, which means quality, attribute, or property), what it means is the pure qualities of the soul*

within us are covered over to varying degrees because of the influence of our physical body and our mind."

Let me conclude this introduction chapter in a simple yet profound way -

If you put off your tasks for a later date, it can affect your productivity in various ways. Many people might believe procrastination is not good, but that's not always the case. Sometimes, delaying tasks can be a good thing. But in many cases, procrastination can lead to increased feelings of fear, low confidence, anxiety, panic, and self-doubt.

In this book, I'll provide 7 powerful hacks to help you get closer to a single, straightforward goal. *You can increase your understanding of procrastination and learn to overcome it, or at the very least, deal with it more successfully by paying attention to these hacks in this book.*

Let me give you a quick rundown of all you will learn from this book:

- ***HACK #1 - DO YOU THINK YOU ARE A PROCRASTINATOR?***

You will know that nobody in this world has a procrastination problem! Yes, you heard it right! Even if you also don't have it. You will find out that it is always the symptom of a problem than the problem itself. This hack will explain that procrastination has nothing to do with your job or work. In my words, procrastination is the most prominent form of stress relief!

- ***HACK #2 - PROCRASTINATION AWARENESS AT ITS CORE***

*This will teach you that you are not alone if you think you are a procrastinator! Even the most famous and great people sometimes struggle with this habit. This will also teach you why we procrastinate, the habit loop, and the biology behind procrastination. You will also learn about the **11 fundamental trigger points** that activate your procrastination loop.*

- ***HACK #3 - The 12 Golden Rules***

*This is one of my favorites and the essential hacks you will learn through this book. It teaches you why you should accept and acknowledge your procrastination. It also talks about the "why" factor of procrastination. Another vital aspect it covers is - "**the 12 golden rules** to handling your procrastination gracefully."*

- ***HACK #4 - CLEAN UP YOUR MIND***

*This will teach you how and why you should take your time to understand your mind and clean it up to eliminate your procrastination habit. It also talks about my favorite **4-step method** that is super helpful in keeping our minds decluttered.*

- ***HACK #5 - KEEP YOUR DREAD AT BAY***

It is important to understand that ***"you are not lazy; you are just afraid!"*** *This is what this hack is all about. You will learn how fear influences procrastination and how you can overcome your fear.*

- ***HACK #6 - SET UP YOUR SMART GOALS TO BEAT PROCRASTINATION***

This hack teaches how to overcome procrastination by understanding and to set ***SMART*** *goals. This also helps you understand why you should have specific, measurable, realistic, and time-bound goals. It also provides a* ***SMART goal template*** *to help you set your goals efficiently and effectively. In detail, this hack explains various techniques, like* **Pomodoro ®, 52/17**, *etc.*

- ***HACK #7 - YOUR CONSISTENCY CAN MAKE IT FOR SURE***

Yes, consistency is the key, and you can use it well to say goodbye to your procrastination. But how to remain consistent, what are the tips and tricks, etc., all these are covered in this hack. Finally, it talks about the positive side of moderate procrastination also. You'll learn that putting things off can also improve your performance if you do it right!

Hope this sounds good. If yes, let's start right now rather than procrastinate any longer.

-- End of Preview --

GET YOUR COPY OF THE COMPLETE BOOK BY SCANNING THE BELOW QR CODE:

Other Books From The Author

Book 1 >> SELF-MOTIVATION like CRAZY: *Increase Your Self-motivation, Learn About the Motivators & Practice 3 Magical Techniques Daily to Eliminate Negative Thoughts & Remain Self-motivated*

Book 2 >> from NIGHT-OWL to MORNING-LARK: *Learn to Wake up Early Like High Achievers to Own YOUR Morning & Practice the Not-So-Obvious Secrets to Elevate YOUR life*

Book 3 >> manifest WEALTH & ABUNDANCE as you read: *Stop Thinking About Your Money Problems, Upgrade Your Mindset with the Power of THANK YOU, &*

Embrace the Process of Giving the Money, Not Just Receiving It!

Book 4 >> Immediate Action: *7 Proven Hacks to Declutter Your Mind & Overcome Procrastination, Master Your Time & Get More Done in Less*

Book 5 >> The Art of Saying NO: *Learn To Stand Up For Yourself, Communicate Effectively, Set Healthy Boundaries, And Be Assertive To Protect Your Happiness*

THANK YOU, READER, FOR SHOWING YOUR TRUST IN ME AND PURCHASING THIS BOOK.

SCAN THE BELOW QR CODE TO JOIN MY NEERA COMMUNITY

SCAN ME

YOUR FREE GIFT

As a token of my thanks for taking out time to read my book, I would like to offer you a FREE gift:

Scan the below QR code & Receive your **FREE BOOK** - ***31 Most Powerful Thoughts For The Day To Bring Self-Transformation In You.***

www.ingramcontent.com/pod-product-compliance
Lightning Source LLC
LaVergne TN
LVHW090355210926
848480LV00002B/345